Data Manipulation in R

Steph Locke (Locke Data)

Contents

About this book

Welcome to the second book in Steph Locke's R Fundamentals series! This second book takes you through how to do manipulation of tabular data in R.

Tabular data is the most commonly encountered data structure we encounter so being able to tidy up the data we receive, summarise it, and combine it with other datasets are vital skills that we all need to be effective at analysing data.

This book will follow the data pipeline from getting data in to R, manipulating it, to then writing it back out for consumption. We'll primarily be using capabilities from the set of packages called the tidyverse[1] within the book.

The book is aimed at beginners to R who understand the basics (check out the Prerequisites) but if you're coming from a coding background or coming back to this book after using R for a while, there is advanced content in many of the chapters. The advanced sections are entirely optional so don't worry if you're just starting to learn R – you don't need those bits just yet but will super-charge your skills when you're ready for them.

Data Manipulation in R by Stephanie Locke is licensed under a Creative Commons Attribution-NonCommercial-ShareAlike 4.0 In-

---

[1]http://tidyverse.org

Figure 1

ternational License.

Feedback

Please let me and others know what you thought of the book by leaving a review on Amazon!

Reviews are vital for me as a writer since it provides me with extra insight that I can apply to future books. Reviews are vital to other people as it gives insight into whether the book is right for them.

If you want to provide feedback outside of the review mechanism for things like errata, suggested future titles etc. you can. Use bit.ly/ldbookfeedback[2] to provide us with information.

---

[2]`http://bit.ly/ldbookfeedback`

Conventions

Throughout this book various conventions will be used.

In terms of basic formatting:

- This is standard text.
- `This is code or a symbol`
- Keyboard keys will be shown like `Ctrl`+`⇧`+`F` ctrl + shift + F
- **This is the first time I mention something important**

This is a book about coding, so expect code blocks. Code blocks will typically look like this:

```
"this is a code block"
```

Directly underneath it, normally starting with two hash symbols (`##`) is the result of the code executing.

```
## [1] "this is a code block"
```

There will also be callouts throughout the book. Some are for information, some expect you to do things.

 Anything written here should be read carefully before proceeding.

This is a tip relating to what I've just said.

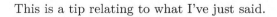

This is kind of like a tip but is for when you're getting into trouble and need help.

 This is something I recommend you do as you're reading.

 This let's you know that something I mention briefly will be followed up on later, whether in this book or a later one.

If you're reading the book in print format, there are often blank pages between chapters – use these to keep notes! The book is to help you learn, not stay pristine.

Prequisites

What you need to already know

This book assumes knowledge of R that covers:

- using functions and packages
- working with vectors
- extracting data out of data.frames

You should be able to say what these lines of code mean:

- `LETTERS[LETTERS>"J"]`
- `iris[, c("Sepal.Length","Species")]`
- `iris$Avg.Petal.Width <- mean(iris$Petal.Width)`
- `list(element=LETTERS)[["element"]]`

If any of the above terms or code are unfamiliar, I recommend you read the first book in the series, Working with R[3].

A basic knowledge of data wrangling will come in handy, but isn't required. You will find this book particularly easy to understand if you can write SQL.

System requirements

You will need R, RStudio, and, if on Windows, Rtools. You can code online at r-fiddle.org[4] but this might be unreliable.

---

[3]`http://geni.us/workingwithr`
[4]`http://www.r-fiddle.org/`

- Install R from r-project.org[5]
- Install Rtools from r-project.org[6]
- Install RStudio from rstudio.com[7]

You should also install the following packages for R:

- `tidyverse`
- `ggplot2movies`
- `nycflights13`
- `odbc`
- `writexl`
- `openxlsx`
- `gapminder`

```
install.packages(c("tidyverse","ggplot2movies",
                   "nycflights13","odbc",
                   "writexl", "openxlsx",
                   "gapminder"))
```

---

[5]https://cloud.r-project.org/
[6]https://cloud.r-project.org/bin/windows/Rtools/
[7]https://www.rstudio.com/products/rstudio/download/#download

About the author

Steph Locke

I am a Microsoft Data Platform MVP with over a decade of business intelligence and data science experience.

Having worked in a variety of industries (including finance, utilities, insurance, and cyber-security,) I've tackled a wide range of business challenges with data. I was awarded the MVP Data Platform award from Microsoft, as a result of organising training and sharing my knowledge with the technical community.

I have a broad background in the Microsoft Data Platform and Azure, but I'm equally conversant with open source tools; from databases like MySQL and PostgreSQL, to analytical languages like R and Python.

Follow me on Twitter via @SteffLocke

Locke Data

I founded Locke Data, an education focused consultancy, to help people get the most out of their data. Locke Data aims to help organisations gain the necessary skills and experience needed to build a successful data science capability, while supporting them on their journey to better data science.

Find out more about Locke Data at itsalocke.com[8].

---

[8]https://itsalocke.com/company/aboutus/

Acknowledgements

This book could not be possible without the skills of Oz Locke. My husband he may be, but most importantly he's a fantastic editor and graphic designer.

I'd like to thank Lise Vaudor for allowing me to include some of her fantastic graphics. Check out her stuff at perso.ens-lyon.fr/lise.vaudor[9].

As well as Oz and Lise, the book would be nowhere as good as it is without the thoughtful feedback provided by these great people:

- Robert Pressau
- Alyssa Columbus
- Dmytro (@dmi3k)
- Paula Jennings
- Jacob Barnett
- Nico Botes

Any errors are my own but Oz and my feedback group have helped me make substantially less of them. Thank you!

---

[9]http://perso.ens-lyon.fr/lise.vaudor/

tidyverse

This book uses `tidyverse` functionality almost exclusively. The `tidyverse` is a collection of packages that share common interface standards and expectations about how you should structure and manipulate your data.

This has advantages because you can spend more time on the concepts and less time working out syntax. It is tremendously powerful for analysts and I think it is a great starting point for people new to coding.

It would be remiss of me to not point out its disadvantages. The guiding ethos emphasises readability not performance. The `tidyverse` performs well for the majority of analytical purposes, however, it may not be fast enough for a particularly demanding production system. In such cases, there is usually a solution out there in base R or another package that will execute faster. If you need high performance R code, you will need to advance beyond this book and I would recommend you read Efficient R Programming[10] by Colin Gillespie. The other significant issue is that the `tidyverse` is expanding[11] and evolving – techniques included in the book may be superseded by newer techniques. The Kindle version will stay up to date so if you've got the book in print, don't forget you can get the Kindle version for free.

Packages from the `tidyverse` that we'll be using throughout are:

- `readr` and `readxl` provide connections to files
- `DBI` provides the basic interface to databases

---

[10] `http://geni.us/effrprog`
[11] Pun intended!

17

- `magrittr` gives the ability to build data pipelines that are very readable
- `dplyr` provides the core tabular manipulation syntax
- `tidyr` allows us to pivot and unpivot our data
- `stringr`, `forcats`, and `lubridate` help us work with text and date columns
- `purrr` helps us work with lists and we'll use this to help do nifty stuff along the way

```
library(tidyverse)
```

Chapter 1

Getting data

This chapter will take you through some of the core packages that allow you to get data into R. It is not exhaustive as there are huge amounts of file types, systems, and APIs that R can work with. There will be a more exhaustive book on this later, but for now I want to get you up to speed with some of the most common data stores.

1.1 Rstudio import wizard

A way to get started importing data from different sources is to use RStudio's import wizard. You can use it to prepare your import and then grab the code to be able to reproduce it later.

To import data...

1. Go to the Environment tab and select Import Dataset
2. Select the relevant type of data you want to import
3. Browse to the file you want to upload.

 Keeping data in the project directory is ideal as it keeps everything in one place and makes imported code easier to read.

1.2 CSVs

The core package we can use for working with CSVs is `readr`, which is loaded by default when we load the `tidyverse`. `readr` is useful for CSVs but it's also good for other flat file formats so if CSV isn't quite what you need, there are also read and write functions for:

- any text file
- log files
- tab or some other delimited file

```
library(readr)
```

> If you have a heavily restricted environment, you may need to make do without being able to use `readr`. In such a situation, you can use `read.csv()` and `write.csv()`, however these are slower and have defaults that mean you usually need to do some tweaking and therefore write more code.
>
> If you have to read or write a lot of data (think hundreds of thousands of records) then you may want to consider the package `data.table` for its `fwrite()` and `fread()` functions that are high performance read and write functions.

The function for reading a CSV is `read_csv()` and by default you only need to provide a file name.

`read_csv()` will try to detect the correct data types for data in the CSV and read the data into a data.frame such that it matches those best guesses. Note that `read_csv()` does not automatically assign the resulting dataset into memory so you need to assign it into memory.

```
iris2 <- read_csv("iris.csv")
```

```
## Parsed with column specification:
## cols(
##   Sepal.Length = col_double(),
##   Sepal.Width = col_double(),
##   Petal.Length = col_double(),
##   Petal.Width = col_double(),
```

```
##    Species = col_character()
## )
```

Arguments that you can use if you need to tweak the settings are:

- `col_names` means that you can provide (alternative) column names for the resulting data.frame.
  - If you're making alternatives make sure to set the `skip` argument so that it ignores existing header rows.
- `col_types` allows to define the datatypes instead of relying on `readr` determining them.
  - `readr` contains a number of `col_*()` functions that allow you to assess what datatype a column should be.
  - A great place to start is with the column specification that gets printed out as a message when you read in the CSV as this tells you the starting setup.
- `locale` allows you to specify a different locale using `locale()` so that you can read in data with commas as decimal marks for instance.
- `na` allows you to provide a vector of values that you want converted to NA in your dataset.
- `quoted_na` is a boolean set by default to TRUE such that if it sees "NA" in a CSV it will read that as an NA not the string "NA".
- `quote` allows to provide the string delimiter if it's not the standard speech mark.
- `comment` allows you to handle situations where people have put comments in CSVs.
- `trim_ws` will remove excess white space at the beginning and end of values and is defaulted to TRUE.
- `skip` says how many lines to skip when reading the data in. This is useful when you want to skip the header row or the data doesn't start at line 1.
- `n_max` provides a limit as to the number of rows that will be read by `read_csv()`. The default is to read all the rows.
- `guess_max` provides `read_csv()` with the number of rows (from the top of the file) it should be used to determine datatype. The default is a thousand records.
- `progress` will give progress updates if the dataset is large in an interactive setting like running some code in RStudio. You can set it FALSE to prevent excess messages.

```
iris2<-read_csv("iris.csv",
            col_names = c("sepal_length","sepal_width",
            "petal_length","petal_width",
            "species"),
                skip=1)
```

```
## Parsed with column specification:
## cols(
##   sepal_length = col_double(),
##   sepal_width = col_double(),
##   petal_length = col_double(),
##   petal_width = col_double(),
##   species = col_character()
## )
```

sepal_length	sepal_width	petal_length	petal_width	species
5.1	3.5	1.4	0.2	setosa
4.9	3.0	1.4	0.2	setosa
4.7	3.2	1.3	0.2	setosa
4.6	3.1	1.5	0.2	setosa
5.0	3.6	1.4	0.2	setosa
5.4	3.9	1.7	0.4	setosa

You can alternatively use `read_delim()`, `read_csv2`, or `read_tsv()` for similarly structured data but with different delimiters.

1.3   Spreadsheets

The best way to read spreadsheets at the moment is with the `readxl` package, that is part of the`tidyverse`. It will work with both ".xls" and ".xlsx" files which is great because there are still tools and processes spitting out files with ".xls" extensions a decade after it went out of use in Microsoft Office.

```
library(readxl)
```

The `read_excel()` function will find a table of data on the first sheet of a workbook. This means it'll ignore most headers and give a good read experience straight away.

```
iris2 <- read_excel("iris.xlsx")
```

You can specify the sheet to read data from using the **sheet** argument. You may want to first get a list of sheets you might need to read from. **readxl** provides **excel_sheets()** for this task.

```
excel_sheets("iris.xlsx")
```

[1] "Sheet1"

The **read_excel()** function's optional arguments are very similar to those of **read_csv()** so I won't repeat them. The main difference of note is that **read_excel()** will also accept a **range** argument so that you can specify a range (including a sheet name) of cells to read.

```
iris2 <- read_excel("iris.xlsx",
        col_names = c("sepal_length","sepal_width",
        "petal_length","petal_width",
        "species"),
        skip=1)
```

sepal_length	sepal_width	petal_length	petal_width	species
5.1	3.5	1.4	0.2	setosa
4.9	3.0	1.4	0.2	setosa
4.7	3.2	1.3	0.2	setosa
4.6	3.1	1.5	0.2	setosa
5.0	3.6	1.4	0.2	setosa
5.4	3.9	1.7	0.4	setosa

1.4 Advanced reading of data

Sometimes, we don't just want to read data from one file, tab, or table but multiple files, tabs, or tables. In such circumstances, we might not even know the names of all the files we want to work with or there may be too many names to work with. Reading and combining that data could be tough were it not for **purrr**.

purrr contains functions that allow us to work with lists. In practice we can handle anything as a list including a vector of filenames, for instance. The **map()** function and type-specific variants come in very handy as they allow us to run another function against each element in our list.

This means that we can use **map()** to apply one of the functions for reading in data against every file so that all files get read into memory. If all the results are tabular then we can even the use the data.frame specific version of **map()**, **map_df()**, to immediately collapse everything into one big dataset.

map() and **map_df()** take two key inputs. The first is the list (or vector) that we want to process. The second is the name of the function we want to run against each item in the list. The function name doesn't need brackets after it as **purrr** will grab the code for the function and execute it for us. We only need brackets when we're going to execute the function ourselves.

Super handily for us, the **map_df()** function will also cope with different column names and data types when it combines them. Data gets matched by column name[1] and where there's not a match a new column will be made. If the column datatypes change over files then the column will end up as safest column type for all the data encountered. This makes this technique excellent for combining data that could vary.[2]

```
map_df(
  list.files(pattern="*.csv"),
  read_csv)
```

---

[1]So provide column names if you have a default set you always want adhered to

[2]If you've used ETL tools like SQL Server Integration Services you'll know that such tools usually have a fixed metadata concept so new or missing columns can really break things. R is much better for dynamic ETL challenges I've found.

Sepal.Width	Petal.Length	Petal.Width	Species	Sepal.Length
3.5	1.4	0.2	setosa	NA
3.0	1.4	0.2	setosa	NA
3.2	1.3	0.2	setosa	NA
3.1	1.5	0.2	setosa	NA
3.6	1.4	0.2	setosa	NA
3.9	1.7	0.4	setosa	NA

1.5 Databases

DBI provides an interface for working with lots of different databases. There's a lot of change right now that's seeing many R packages that work with specific databases being overhauled. Instead of using a specific database package, I like to use the odbc package these days as most databases have an ODBC driver.

The RStudio site on working with databases is pretty nifty! db.rstudio.com

```
library(DBI)
library(odbc)
```

To work with a database you'll need a copy of the ODBC driver installed on your system. You can then use this to connect to databases that are compatible with that driver. Here I'm going to use the SQL Server ODBC Driver[3] as it is cross-platform compatible and Redgate[4] provide a database that anyone can connect to for practicing their SQL writing skills. When connecting to your own database you typically need to know the following:

- exact driver name
- server name
- database name[5]
- login credentials
- port number that the database allows you connect over

---

[3]https://docs.microsoft.com/en-us/sql/connect/odbc/download-odbc-driver-for-sql-server

[4]https://www.red-gate.com/

[5]The name of the specific database not whether it's MySQL etc.

You then need to feed these bits of information into the function `dbConnect()` along with the R function that covers your driver – in our case that's simply `odbc()`.

```
dbConn<-dbConnect(odbc(),
          driver="ODBC Driver 13 for SQL Server",
          server="mhknbn2kdz.database.windows.net",
          database="AdventureWorks2012",
          uid="sqlfamily",
          pwd="sqlf@m1ly")
```

Once you have this connection object, you can then use it to interface with the database.

If we want to write some SQL against the database to retrieve some data, we use `dbGetQuery()` function which takes a database connection object and some SQL in a string.

```
transactions <- dbGetQuery(
          dbConn,
          "select *
          from Production.TransactionHistory")
```

You can also grab an entire table into R using `dbFetchTable()`[6]. If the table is very large I would not recommend doing this and would recommend `dbGetQuery()` instead as you can provide filters.

```
sqlfamily <- dbReadTable(dbConn, "SqlFamily")
```

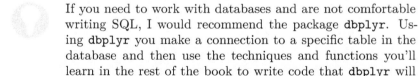

If you need to work with databases and are not comfortable writing SQL, I would recommend the package `dbplyr`. Using `dbplyr` you make a connection to a specific table in the database and then use the techniques and functions you'll learn in the rest of the book to write code that `dbplyr` will then translate into SQL that it will send to the database to run.

---

[6]Subject to the limitation of working within the default schema at present.

1.6 Summary

There are numerous packages for reading data from various sources. In this brief chapter we covered how to read CSV, Excel, and a database. The packages I recommend you get started with are `readr`, `readxl`, `DBI`, and `odbc`. This chapter is rudimentary and more in-depth coverage of working with these data sources and others will be in a later book.

Chapter 2

Data pipelines

Once you have some the data, we next need to start processing it. In the past, you would often see data pipelines that looked like:

```
# The all-in-one
avg_area<-mean(iris$Sepal.Length[iris$Species=="setosa"]*
              iris$Sepal.Width[iris$Species=="setosa"])

# One assign at a time
is_setosa    <- iris$Species=="setosa"
setosa       <- iris[is_setosa, ]
setosa_area <- setosa$Sepal.Length * setosa$Sepal.Width
avg_area     <- mean(setosa_area)
```

The all-in-one approach is a set of nested functions and logic that means you need to spend time finding the innermost actions and work out from there. If you've used Excel you probably have flashbacks to horribly complicated nested formulae!

Doing things in smaller steps and assigning them along the way means we can see what's going on more effectively. It's very handy for someone to read but all those assignments could make it very difficult for us to work if we're working with large datasets or a small amount of memory.

Enter **piping**.

Piping allows us to create series of connected transformations that

Figure 2.1

goes from the source to the destination. Instead of nesting functions you hook them together like pieces of plumbing so that your data passes through them and changes as it goes.

This has the benefit of nested functions in that it puts less things into memory and it also has the benefit of the step by step assign approach as it doesn't involve any nested functions. If you've written bash, PowerShell, C# fluent, F# or other functional programming languages you will find this easy to adopt.

2.1   About piping in R

The pipe operator was first designed and implemented in R by Stefan Milton Bache in the package `magrittr`[1]. Created in 2014, it is now very heavily used and its widest adoption has been within the `tidyverse`. This book and many of the future ones will rely heavily on packages in the `tidyverse` to help you write R code that does awesome things.

When we write R code using pipes we'll do things step by step and refer to the pipe operator as *then* when we say it out loud e.g. "get the iris data *then* filter to setosa records *then* create an area column *then* calculate the average".

To perform this piping we have a special operator, `%>%`[2], that we use between functions.[3]

---

[1]`magrittr` is named after René Magritte and plays on his piece of art called *The Treachery of Images.*

[2]The short cut in RStudio is `Ctrl`+`M` Ctrl + M

[3]There are other pipe operators in the `magrittr` package but these are rarely required in my experience.

```
library(magrittr)
```

2.2 Simple usage

Let's take some R code `length(toupper(letters))` and translate it into a pipeline. We work out what the innermost part is and then work our way outwards. Doing this, we get:

1. Get the `letters` object
2. Apply the `toupper()` function to `letters`
3. Count the results using `length()`

In pipelines you put the starting object first and then apply the functions sequentially with a pipe (`%>%`) between each one. A pipeline can sit on a single line or be split out to show one instruction per line. As the pipe basically says "take what you've calculated and pass it along" it handily makes it the first input by default, so we don't even have to do anything in a lot of cases except keep adding functions to our pipeline.

```
letters %>%
  toupper() %>%
  length()
```

```
## [1] 26
```

Now, let's go the other way and translate a pipeline into nested functions.

```
iris %>%
  head() %>%
  nrow()
```

```
## [1] 6
```

1. Get the `iris` dataset
2. Take some rows from the top of the dataset
3. Count how many rows are in the subset

This would be `nrow(head(iris))`. These are fairly trivial examples but we'll see much bigger pipelines later.

2.3   Assigning results

Pipelines are compatible with assigning to memory in a variety of ways. You can still assign using a left hand side (LHS) operator.

```
iris_filtered <- iris %>% head()

iris_filtered2 <- iris %>%
  head()
```

However, because of the way data pipelines flow from top to bottom and left to right it feels somewhat counter-intuitive to have the output and input on the same line. As a result, when I use data pipelines I make use of the right hand side (RHS) operator ->.

```
iris %>%
  head() ->
  iris_filtered3
```

Note that you do not have to use the brackets after a functions' name if you're not providing any further inputs. This would make your code shorter, but at the point of writing this, such code will throw errors when you convert your code into a package. Whilst it might be a long time between now and when you write your first package, the habit of using brackets will save you problems down the line.

These feel more natural to me and I'll use them throughout. Like most things in R, there is no single right way, but there's definitely my way!

2.4 Jumbled functions

Sometimes functions that we encounter do not put the key input as the first argument. Here are some examples:

```
# The input vector is the last thing you supply to sub()
letterz <- sub("s","z", letters)

# Statistical modelling functions usually take a
# description of the model first before you provide
# the training dataset
my_lm <- lm(Sepal.Width~Sepal.Length, iris)
```

By default, our pipelines will put our objects as the first input to a function. To work with these jumbled functions we need a way to tell our pipelines where to use our input instead of relying on the defaults. The way we can do that is with a period (.). By using this as a place holder for a given arguments input we can put our data anywhere in a function. Our two examples thus become:

```
letters %>%
  sub("s","z", .) ->
  letterz

iris %>%
  lm(Sepal.Width~Sepal.Length, .) ->
  my_lm
```

2.5 Summary

Build data pipelines using the %>% operator that is available from **magrittr**, **tidyverse**, or reimplemented in many R packages.

Pipelines put the results of the previous code into the first argument of the next piece of code. The default behaviour can be modified by using a . to denote where the input should go. Assigning the results of a pipeline to an object can be done by using the -> operator.

2.6 Exercises

1. Write a pipeline that samples from the vector **LETTERS** 200 times and stores the result in a vector called `lots_of_LETTERS`
2. Write a pipeline that provides upper-cased versions of the column names of the dataset `mtcars`

Chapter 3

Filtering columns

To extract columns from our dataset, we can use the `select()` function to provide instructions about which columns we want or don't want. `select()` takes a comma separated list of instructions.

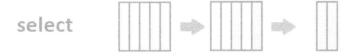

select

3.1 Basic selections

The most basic `select()` is one where you comma separate a list of columns you want included. If you need to refer to tricky column names with spaces or other things that break the standard naming conventions, you use back ticks (') to enclose the column name.

```
iris %>%
  select(Species, Sepal.Length)
```

Species	Sepal.Length
setosa	5.1
setosa	4.9
setosa	4.7
setosa	4.6
setosa	5.0
setosa	5.4

If we have lots of columns we want to include but a few we want to exclude, we can use a minus (-) before a column name to say to exclude it.

```
iris %>%
  select(-Species)
```

Sepal.Length	Sepal.Width	Petal.Length	Petal.Width
5.1	3.5	1.4	0.2
4.9	3.0	1.4	0.2
4.7	3.2	1.3	0.2
4.6	3.1	1.5	0.2
5.0	3.6	1.4	0.2
5.4	3.9	1.7	0.4

We can provide a range of columns to return two columns and everything in between. This uses syntax like generating a sequence of numbers incrementing by 1 e.g. 1:5. These can be comma separated too, and also work with referencing specific columns.

```
iris %>%
  select(Sepal.Length:Petal.Length)
```

Sepal.Width	Petal.Length	Petal.Width
3.5	1.4	0.2
3.0	1.4	0.2
3.2	1.3	0.2
3.1	1.5	0.2
3.6	1.4	0.2
3.9	1.7	0.4

Using the minus symbol to exclude a column can also combine with the range capability to exclude a range of columns.

```
iris %>%
  select(-(Sepal.Length:Petal.Length))
```

Sepal.Length	Species
5.1	setosa
4.9	setosa
4.7	setosa
4.6	setosa
5.0	setosa
5.4	setosa

Note that if you exclude a column and include it later in the same select(), the column will not be excluded. If you exclude a column after including it in a select(), the column will be excluded.

```
iris %>%
  select(-Species, Species)
```

Sepal.Length	Sepal.Width	Petal.Length	Petal.Width	Species
5.1	3.5	1.4	0.2	setosa
4.9	3.0	1.4	0.2	setosa
4.7	3.2	1.3	0.2	setosa
4.6	3.1	1.5	0.2	setosa
5.0	3.6	1.4	0.2	setosa
5.4	3.9	1.7	0.4	setosa

```
iris %>%
  select(Sepal.Width, Species, -Species)
```

Sepal.Width
3.5
3.0
3.2
3.1
3.6
3.9

3.2   Name-based selection

There are a number of helper functions that can allow us to include (or exclude) columns based on their names.

- `starts_with()` will return columns where the string you provide is at the beginning of a column name
- `ends_with()` will return columns where the string you provide is at the end of a column name
- `contains()` will return columns where the string you provide is anywhere in the column name
- `num_range()` will allow you to return columns with names like "Sales 2014" through to "Sales 2017" by providing a prefix and a numeric range you want to select
- `matches()` allows you to provide pattern that a column name must conform to in order to be returned
- `one_of()` allows you to provide a vector of column names (perhaps as a result of user input) that you would like to be matched in their entirety

```
iris %>%
  select(starts_with("S"))
```

Sepal.Length	Sepal.Width	Species
5.1	3.5	setosa
4.9	3.0	setosa
4.7	3.2	setosa
4.6	3.1	setosa
5.0	3.6	setosa
5.4	3.9	setosa

```
iris %>%
  select(ends_with("s"))
```

Species
setosa
setosa
setosa
setosa
setosa
setosa

```
iris %>%
  select(contains("Length"))
```

Sepal.Length	Petal.Length
5.1	1.4
4.9	1.4
4.7	1.3
4.6	1.5
5.0	1.4
5.4	1.7

These can be used in `select()` statements with column names, exclusions, and ranges.

```
iris %>%
  select(Petal.Width:Species, -contains("Length"))
```

Petal.Width	Species
0.2	setosa
0.2	setosa
0.2	setosa
0.2	setosa
0.2	setosa
0.4	setosa

3.3 Content based selection

You can also select columns based on the boolean results of functions applied to the data in the columns. We can use `select_if()` to supply some criteria that relates to the data. When we reference

functions to be used by `select_if()` we don't include brackets after the function names because `select_if()` needs to take the
function and apply it to every column.[1]

For instance, if we wanted all numeric columns from the `iris`
dataset we can use `is.numeric()` to check out each column of
data and return a boolean if the data is numeric or not.

```
iris %>%
  select_if(is.numeric)
```

Sepal.Length	Sepal.Width	Petal.Length	Petal.Width
5.1	3.5	1.4	0.2
4.9	3.0	1.4	0.2
4.7	3.2	1.3	0.2
4.6	3.1	1.5	0.2
5.0	3.6	1.4	0.2
5.4	3.9	1.7	0.4

3.4   Advanced conditional selection

Existing functions don't always fit your requirements when you
want to specify which columns you want.

You can create conditional statements on the fly by using a tilde
(~) and then providing some code that results in a boolean. You
tell the statement where the column of data should go by using the
place holder symbol (.).

For instance, what if we wanted only numeric columns with a high
degree of variation? We use the ~ to say we're writing a custom
condition and then do an AND that checks if the column is numeric
and if the number of unique values in the column is more than 30.

```
iris %>%
  select_if(~is.numeric(.) & n_distinct(.)>30)
```

---

[1]By not including brackets we're saying use the function denoted by this
name as opposed to instructing it to execute the function denoted by this
name.

Sepal.Length	Petal.Length
5.1	1.4
4.9	1.4
4.7	1.3
4.6	1.5
5.0	1.4
5.4	1.7

If you're going to reuse your condition in multiple situations, you can extract it and use `as_mapper()` to turn some code you've already written into a function.[2]

```
is_v_unique_num <- as_mapper(
  ~is.numeric(.) & n_distinct(.)>30
  )
```

This can be used in a standalone fashion or within your `*_if()` functions.

```
is_v_unique_num(1:5)
is_v_unique_num(LETTERS)
is_v_unique_num(1:50)
```

```
## [1] FALSE
## [1] FALSE
## [1] TRUE
```

```
iris %>%
  select_if(is_highly_unique_number)
```

Sepal.Length	Petal.Length
5.1	1.4
4.9	1.4
4.7	1.3
4.6	1.5
5.0	1.4
5.4	1.7

---

[2]If you haven't already written the code then you have a great range of choices including the more traditional way of specifying a function which is `function(){}`. Function writing will be covered in a later book.

3.5   Summary

We can produce subsets of columns from datasets very easily using
`select()` and variants like `select_if()`.

`select()` allows us to refer to columns that we want to be included
or excluded in a variety of ways.

- Individual columns can be included using their names
- Exclude individual columns by prefixing the column name
  with a -
- Refer to range of columns by using a : between the first and
  last column you want retried
- Perform a string match to retrieve columns
    - Use `starts_with()` to match columns based on what
      they start with
    - Use `ends_with()` to match columns based on what they
      end with
    - Use `contains()` to match columns based on if they con-
      tain a string
    - Use `matches()` to match columns based on a pattern
    - Use `one_of()` to match columns based on a vector of
      desired columns
    - Use `num_range()` to match columns that have an incre-
      menting numeric value in the name

Use `select_if()` to provide a condition based on the contents of
the column, not the name.

3.6   Exercises

1. Write a `select()` that gets from the `movies` data (from
   `ggplot2movies`) the columns `title` through to `votes`, and
   `Action` through to `Short`
2. Write a query that brings back the `movies` dataset without
   any column that begins with `r` or `m`
3. [ADVANCED] Write a query that returns columns that have
   a high degree of missing data (more than 25% of rows are
   NA) from the `movies` dataset

Chapter 4

Filtering rows

Filtering out rows we don't want in our data or selecting only the ones we're interested in for a given piece of analysis is important. This section takes you through how to tackle these tasks.

4.1   Row-position selection

To select records from our datasets based on where they appear, we can use the function `slice()`. The `slice()` function takes a vector of values that denote positions. These can be positive values for inclusion or negative values for exclusion.

```
iris %>%
  slice(1:5)
```

Sepal.Length	Sepal.Width	Petal.Length	Petal.Width	Species
5.1	3.5	1.4	0.2	setosa
4.9	3.0	1.4	0.2	setosa
4.7	3.2	1.3	0.2	setosa
4.6	3.1	1.5	0.2	setosa
5.0	3.6	1.4	0.2	setosa

There's a helpful function `n()`, which returns the row count, that makes it easy to construct queries that are based on the number of rows.

```
iris %>%
  slice(-(1:floor(n()/3)))
```

Sepal.Length	Sepal.Width	Petal.Length	Petal.Width	Species
7.0	3.2	4.7	1.4	versicolor
6.4	3.2	4.5	1.5	versicolor
6.9	3.1	4.9	1.5	versicolor
5.5	2.3	4.0	1.3	versicolor
6.5	2.8	4.6	1.5	versicolor
5.7	2.8	4.5	1.3	versicolor

4.2   Conditional selection

It's pretty rare that we want to just select by row number though.
Usually, we want to use some sort of logical statement. These filters
say which rows to include if they meet the condition in our logical
statement i.e. the condition evaluates to TRUE for the row. The
function we can use to select rows based on a logical statement is
`filter()`.

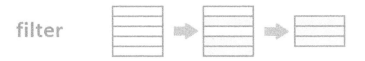

```
iris %>%
  filter(Species=="virginica")
```

Sepal.Length	Sepal.Width	Petal.Length	Petal.Width	Species
6.3	3.3	6.0	2.5	virginica
5.8	2.7	5.1	1.9	virginica
7.1	3.0	5.9	2.1	virginica
6.3	2.9	5.6	1.8	virginica
6.5	3.0	5.8	2.2	virginica
7.6	3.0	6.6	2.1	virginica

Instead of needing to write multiple `filter()` commands, we can put multiple logical conditions inside a single `filter()` function. You can comma separate conditions, which is equivalent to an "AND", or you can use the compound logical operators "AND" (`&`) and "OR" (`|`) to construct more complex statements.

```
iris %>%
  filter(Species == "virginica",
         Sepal.Length > mean(Sepal.Length))
```

Sepal.Length	Sepal.Width	Petal.Length	Petal.Width	Species
6.3	3.3	6.0	2.5	virginica
7.1	3.0	5.9	2.1	virginica
6.3	2.9	5.6	1.8	virginica
6.5	3.0	5.8	2.2	virginica
7.6	3.0	6.6	2.1	virginica
7.3	2.9	6.3	1.8	virginica

```
iris %>%
  filter(Species == "virginica" |
         Sepal.Length > mean(Sepal.Length))
```

Sepal.Length	Sepal.Width	Petal.Length	Petal.Width	Species
7.0	3.2	4.7	1.4	versicolor
6.4	3.2	4.5	1.5	versicolor
6.9	3.1	4.9	1.5	versicolor
6.5	2.8	4.6	1.5	versicolor
6.3	3.3	4.7	1.6	versicolor
6.6	2.9	4.6	1.3	versicolor

4.3 Advanced row filtering

We can also apply a filter to each column. This enables you to return only rows where the condition is TRUE for all columns (an AND) or where the condition is TRUE for any of the columns (an OR).

We can construct these using `filter_all()`, providing a condition that will be calculated per column for each row, and a requirement about how many conditions need to have been met for a row to be returned.

- Use the place holder (.) to indicate where a column's values should be used in a condition
- The place holder can be used multiple times in a condition
- If the condition must be TRUE for all columns, then we wrap our condition in `all_vars()`
- If only one column needs to return a TRUE then we wrap it in `any_vars()`

Let's try out some examples to see the sorts of filters you can create using these three functions.

- Return any row where a column's value exceeds a specified value

```
iris %>%
  filter_all(any_vars(.>7.5))
```

Sepal.Length	Sepal.Width	Petal.Length	Petal.Width	Species
7.6	3.0	6.6	2.1	virginica
7.7	3.8	6.7	2.2	virginica
7.7	2.6	6.9	2.3	virginica
7.7	2.8	6.7	2.0	virginica
7.9	3.8	6.4	2.0	virginica
7.7	3.0	6.1	2.3	virginica

- Find rows where any column's value is more than two standard deviations away from the mean

```
iris %>%
  filter_all(any_vars(abs(. - mean(.))>2*sd(.)))
```

Sepal.Length	Sepal.Width	Petal.Length	Petal.Width	Species
5.8	4.0	1.2	0.2	setosa
5.7	4.4	1.5	0.4	setosa
5.2	4.1	1.5	0.1	setosa
5.5	4.2	1.4	0.2	setosa
5.0	2.0	3.5	1.0	versicolor
7.6	3.0	6.6	2.1	virginica

If we wanted to do something like finding each row where every numeric column's value was smaller than average, we couldn't write something using `filter_all()` that would work as there's a text column and `mean()` doesn't make sense for text. It would return something that couldn't be interpreted as TRUE and therefore our expectation that all values must be TRUE would never be met.

```
iris %>%
  filter_all(all_vars(. < mean(.)))
```

Sepal.Length	Sepal.Width	Petal.Length	Petal.Width
4.9	3.0	1.4	0.2
4.4	2.9	1.4	0.2
4.8	3.0	1.4	0.1
4.3	3.0	1.1	0.1
5.0	3.0	1.6	0.2
4.4	3.0	1.3	0.2
4.5	2.3	1.3	0.3
4.8	3.0	1.4	0.3
4.9	2.4	3.3	1.0
5.0	2.0	3.5	1.0
5.7	2.6	3.5	1.0
5.5	2.4	3.7	1.0
5.0	2.3	3.3	1.0
5.1	2.5	3.0	1.1

Thankfully, there's a function we can use that will apply a check to each column first, before applying our filter to our rows. Using `filter_if()` we can first provide a column-level condition, and then provide our row-level condition. This enables us to select which columns we want to apply our filter to. The first argument to a `filter_if()` is the name of a function that will return a TRUE or FALSE based on the column's contents. The second argument is the type of filter we've already written in our `filter_all()`.

```
iris %>%
  filter_if(is.numeric, all_vars(.<mean(.)))
```

Sepal.Length	Sepal.Width	Petal.Length	Petal.Width	Species
4.9	3.0	1.4	0.2	setosa
4.4	2.9	1.4	0.2	setosa
4.8	3.0	1.4	0.1	setosa
4.3	3.0	1.1	0.1	setosa
5.0	3.0	1.6	0.2	setosa
4.4	3.0	1.3	0.2	setosa

Sometimes, functions won't already exist for use as column filters. In those instances, we can use custom conditions by using a tilde (~) and our data place holder (.).

```
iris %>%
  filter_if(~is.numeric(.) & n_distinct(.)>30,
            any_vars(.<mean(.)))
```

Sepal.Length	Sepal.Width	Petal.Length	Petal.Width	Species
5.1	3.5	1.4	0.2	setosa
4.9	3.0	1.4	0.2	setosa
4.7	3.2	1.3	0.2	setosa
4.6	3.1	1.5	0.2	setosa
5.0	3.6	1.4	0.2	setosa
5.4	3.9	1.7	0.4	setosa

The final alternative is to apply some criteria to columns that match some given name criteria. To do this, we provide filter_at() with our column criteria in a similar fashion to how we reference them in select() and then we provide the filter condition we then want to apply. filter_at() expects us to group our column selection criteria in one argument so we have to put them in something that groups them together – the mechanism is the function vars() which allows us to provide a comma-separated set of column criteria.

```
iris %>%
  filter_at(vars(ends_with("Length")),
            all_vars(.<mean(.)))
```

Sepal.Length	Sepal.Width	Petal.Length	Petal.Width	Species
5.1	3.5	1.4	0.2	setosa
4.9	3.0	1.4	0.2	setosa
4.7	3.2	1.3	0.2	setosa
4.6	3.1	1.5	0.2	setosa
5.0	3.6	1.4	0.2	setosa
5.4	3.9	1.7	0.4	setosa

4.4 Summary

We can apply filters to our rows in our data set by position using `slice()`, based on applying criteria to specific columns using `filter()`, and programmatically using `filter_all()`, `filter_at()`, and `filter_if()`.

4.5 Exercises

1. Write a filter that gets all action movies from the `movies` dataset via the `ggplot2movies` package
2. Write a filter that removes films lasting more than 6 hours from the `movies` dataset
3. [ADVANCED] Write a filter that checks to see if any of the films don't have any genres flagged at all

Chapter 5

Working with names

5.1 Working with column names

You can rename columns by selecting them but providing a new name on the left-hand side of an equals operator (=) when doing a `select()`. This is useful if you want to filter columns and rename at the same time.

```
iris %>%
  select(sepal_width=Sepal.Width, species=Species)
```

sepal_width	species
3.5	setosa
3.0	setosa
3.2	setosa
3.1	setosa
3.6	setosa
3.9	setosa

If, however, you want to retain all your columns but with some renamed, you can use `rename()` instead. `rename()` will output all columns with the names adjusted.

```
iris %>%
  rename(sepal_width=Sepal.Width, species=Species)
```

Sepal.Length	sepal_width	Petal.Length	Petal.Width	species
5.1	3.5	1.4	0.2	setosa
4.9	3.0	1.4	0.2	setosa
4.7	3.2	1.3	0.2	setosa
4.6	3.1	1.5	0.2	setosa
5.0	3.6	1.4	0.2	setosa
5.4	3.9	1.7	0.4	setosa

5.2 Advanced renaming columns

We can also perform column name changes programmatically by using *_at(), *_if(), and *_all() versions of select() and rename() to change some or all columns. Whether we change some or all, we can provide a transformation function that will alter column names based on some condition.

```
iris %>%
  select_all(str_to_lower)
```

sepal.length	sepal.width	petal.length	petal.width	species
5.1	3.5	1.4	0.2	setosa
4.9	3.0	1.4	0.2	setosa
4.7	3.2	1.3	0.2	setosa
4.6	3.1	1.5	0.2	setosa
5.0	3.6	1.4	0.2	setosa
5.4	3.9	1.7	0.4	setosa

```
iris %>%
  rename_if(is.numeric, str_to_lower)
```

sepal.length	sepal.width	petal.length	petal.width	Species
5.1	3.5	1.4	0.2	setosa
4.9	3.0	1.4	0.2	setosa
4.7	3.2	1.3	0.2	setosa
4.6	3.1	1.5	0.2	setosa
5.0	3.6	1.4	0.2	setosa
5.4	3.9	1.7	0.4	setosa

```
iris %>%
  rename_at(vars(starts_with("S")), str_to_lower)
```

sepal.length	sepal.width	Petal.Length	Petal.Width	species
5.1	3.5	1.4	0.2	setosa
4.9	3.0	1.4	0.2	setosa
4.7	3.2	1.3	0.2	setosa
4.6	3.1	1.5	0.2	setosa
5.0	3.6	1.4	0.2	setosa
5.4	3.9	1.7	0.4	setosa

5.3 Working with row names

Generally speaking you want to avoid creating or working with data.frames that use row names. It makes sense for a matrix to have row names that are meaningful as you wouldn't want to add a text column into your numeric matrix and force everything to text. Encoding important information like IDs into an attribute risks it getting lost or overwritten. We can avoid this risk by adding these into a column. Once row names are converted to a column, if you need to make any amendments you can use the techniques you'll learn later in this book.

The dataset `mtcars` is a dataset with a row per vehicle with the row names containing the car make and model.

```
mtcars
```

	mpg	cyl	disp	hp	drat	wt	qsec	vs
Mazda RX4	21.0	6	160	110	3.90	2.620	16.46	0
Mazda RX4 Wag	21.0	6	160	110	3.90	2.875	17.02	0
Datsun 710	22.8	4	108	93	3.85	2.320	18.61	1
Hornet 4 Drive	21.4	6	258	110	3.08	3.215	19.44	1
Hornet Sportabout	18.7	8	360	175	3.15	3.440	17.02	0
Valiant	18.1	6	225	105	2.76	3.460	20.22	1

We can use the function `rownames_to_column()`[1] to move the row
names into a column and we can (optionally) provide a name for
the new column.

```
mtcars %>%
  rownames_to_column("car")
```

car	mpg	cyl	disp	hp	drat	wt	qsec
Mazda RX4	21.0	6	160	110	3.90	2.620	16.46
Mazda RX4 Wag	21.0	6	160	110	3.90	2.875	17.02
Datsun 710	22.8	4	108	93	3.85	2.320	18.61
Hornet 4 Drive	21.4	6	258	110	3.08	3.215	19.44
Hornet Sportabout	18.7	8	360	175	3.15	3.440	17.02
Valiant	18.1	6	225	105	2.76	3.460	20.22

5.4 Summary

Renaming columns can be performed by using **rename()** or as part
of your **select()** process. Both **rename()** and **select()** have
variants that allow you to amend column names programmatically.

When working with row names in tabular data, my recommendation is to make them into a column in order to be able to amend
them more easily. Use `rownames_to_column()` to do this.

---

[1] `rownames_to_column()` comes from the package **tibble** which is part of the
framework that a lot of the **tidyverse** packages rely upon. It gets loaded by
default when you load the **tidyverse**.

5.5   Exercises

1. Output the `movies` dataset with the column `budget` changed to `budget_if_known`
2. [ADVANCED] Write a query that returns from the `movies` dataset columns that have a high degree of missing data (more than 25% of rows are NA) and upper case all the output column names

Chapter 6

Re-arranging your data

Rearranging a table is something I recommend for output and when you need things ordered to be able to perform some sort of calculation like difference from previous year. Generally, I would keep your data as-is for as a long as possible.

6.1   Sorting rows

To sort your rows, you can use the function **arrange()**. You provide **arrange()** with a comma separated list of columns you wish to sort by, where the first column will be the one sorted, then the second column sorted where the values in the first column are the same, and so on. By default, **arrange()** sorts columns in ascending order i.e. from smallest to largest. To change the sort order to descending for a column you put the function **desc()** around the column name.

```
iris %>%
  arrange(desc(Species), Sepal.Length)
```

Sepal.Length	Sepal.Width	Petal.Length	Petal.Width	Species
4.9	2.5	4.5	1.7	virginica
5.6	2.8	4.9	2.0	virginica
5.7	2.5	5.0	2.0	virginica
5.8	2.7	5.1	1.9	virginica
5.8	2.8	5.1	2.4	virginica
5.8	2.7	5.1	1.9	virginica

6.2   Advanced row sorting

You can also use `arrange_all()`, `arrange_at()`, and `arrange_if()` to provide sorting on the all the data (from left to right) or to sort by columns that meet criteria. You can provide these functions with **desc** as the sort order behaviour you want applied.

```
iris %>%
  arrange_all()
```

Sepal.Length	Sepal.Width	Petal.Length	Petal.Width	Species
4.3	3.0	1.1	0.1	setosa
4.4	2.9	1.4	0.2	setosa
4.4	3.0	1.3	0.2	setosa
4.4	3.2	1.3	0.2	setosa
4.5	2.3	1.3	0.3	setosa
4.6	3.1	1.5	0.2	setosa

```
iris %>%
  arrange_if(is.character, desc)
```

Sepal.Length	Sepal.Width	Petal.Length	Petal.Width	Species
5.1	3.5	1.4	0.2	setosa
4.9	3.0	1.4	0.2	setosa
4.7	3.2	1.3	0.2	setosa
4.6	3.1	1.5	0.2	setosa
5.0	3.6	1.4	0.2	setosa
5.4	3.9	1.7	0.4	setosa

```
iris %>%
  arrange_at(vars(Species, starts_with("P")), desc)
```

Sepal.Length	Sepal.Width	Petal.Length	Petal.Width	Species
7.7	2.6	6.9	2.3	virginica
7.7	3.8	6.7	2.2	virginica
7.7	2.8	6.7	2.0	virginica
7.6	3.0	6.6	2.1	virginica
7.9	3.8	6.4	2.0	virginica
7.3	2.9	6.3	1.8	virginica

6.3 Reordering columns

You can use the `select()` function to re-order columns.

If you want to move some known values you can use the `everything()` function inside your `select()` to denote that you want everything else brought back that hasn't yet been mentioned.

```
iris %>%
  select(starts_with("P"), everything())
```

Petal.Length	Petal.Width	Sepal.Length	Sepal.Width	Species
1.4	0.2	5.1	3.5	setosa
1.4	0.2	4.9	3.0	setosa
1.3	0.2	4.7	3.2	setosa
1.5	0.2	4.6	3.1	setosa
1.4	0.2	5.0	3.6	setosa
1.7	0.4	5.4	3.9	setosa

To sort alphabetically, we need to extract column names which we can do using the function `current_vars()` and then sort the names.

```
iris %>%
  select(sort(current_vars()))
```

Petal.Length	Petal.Width	Sepal.Length	Sepal.Width	Species
1.4	0.2	5.1	3.5	setosa
1.4	0.2	4.9	3.0	setosa
1.3	0.2	4.7	3.2	setosa
1.5	0.2	4.6	3.1	setosa
1.4	0.2	5.0	3.6	setosa
1.7	0.4	5.4	3.9	setosa

6.4   Summary

Use `arrange()` to sort your dataset by known columns. Provide `desc()` to denote when you want to columns to be sorted in descending order. You can sort by all columns using `arrange_all()`, `arrange_at()`, and use `arrange_if()` to sort by columns that match some criteria. Use `select()` to reorder columns.

6.5   Exercises

1. Sort the `movies` data by title in descending order
2. [ADVANCED] Sort the `movies` data by columns containing only two unique values

Chapter 7

Changing your data

This section will focus on how you can update, drop, and create new columns. All of these changes do not occur to the underlying dataset so if you want to update the dataset you need to overwrite it.

To make changes, we `mutate()` our dataset. The `mutate()` function takes any number of expressions that take columns and return new values of the same length.

mutate

The functions we use in the expressions need to work on vectors and operate just like how they would behave if we were working on the vector independently of the data.frame.[1] If we put a name on the LHS of an expression and an = between them, we give the new column a name.

---

[1] The data.frame is a list where each element is an object with the same number of elements as all the others. Consequently, whilst we usually have simple vectors as columns, you can actually have list columns that contain lists or data.frames. You can use `mutate()` to work with these types of columns but they're typically encountered when working with APIs do we'll cover them when we look at working with APIs in a later book.

```
iris %>%
  mutate(Sepal.Area = Sepal.Width * Sepal.Length)
```

Sepal.Length	Petal.Width	Species	Sepal.Area
5.1	0.2	setosa	17.85
4.9	0.2	setosa	14.70
4.7	0.2	setosa	15.04
4.6	0.2	setosa	14.26
5.0	0.2	setosa	18.00
5.4	0.4	setosa	21.06

When using `mutate()` you can create multiple new columns, some of which depend on others being created at the same time. You can also utilise column-level aggregates in your expressions.

```
iris %>%
  mutate(Sepal.Area = Sepal.Width * Sepal.Length,
  Avg.Sepal.Area = mean(Sepal.Area))
```

Sepal.Length	Petal.Width	Species	Sepal.Area	Avg.Sepal.Area
5.1	0.2	setosa	17.85	17.82287
4.9	0.2	setosa	14.70	17.82287
4.7	0.2	setosa	15.04	17.82287
4.6	0.2	setosa	14.26	17.82287
5.0	0.2	setosa	18.00	17.82287
5.4	0.4	setosa	21.06	17.82287

Updating a column involves using its name on the LHS of an assign.

```
iris %>%
  mutate(Sepal.Width=Sepal.Width*.9)
```

Sepal.Length	Sepal.Width	Petal.Length	Petal.Width	Species
5.1	3.15	1.4	0.2	setosa
4.9	2.70	1.4	0.2	setosa
4.7	2.88	1.3	0.2	setosa
4.6	2.79	1.5	0.2	setosa
5.0	3.24	1.4	0.2	setosa
5.4	3.51	1.7	0.4	setosa

To delete a column, you can either assign NULL[2] to a column in a `mutate()` statement or use the exclude syntax for a `select()` statement.

```
iris %>%
  mutate(Sepal.Length=NULL)
```

Sepal.Width	Petal.Length	Petal.Width	Species
3.5	1.4	0.2	setosa
3.0	1.4	0.2	setosa
3.2	1.3	0.2	setosa
3.1	1.5	0.2	setosa
3.6	1.4	0.2	setosa
3.9	1.7	0.4	setosa

```
iris %>%
  select(-Sepal.Width)
```

Sepal.Length	Petal.Length	Petal.Width	Species
5.1	1.4	0.2	setosa
4.9	1.4	0.2	setosa
4.7	1.3	0.2	setosa
4.6	1.5	0.2	setosa
5.0	1.4	0.2	setosa
5.4	1.7	0.4	setosa

New columns, updating existing ones, and dropping columns can all be done in the same `mutate()` function and R will work out the best order to evaluate the various instructions.

Just because you can do something all in one line, doesn't necessarily mean you should. It can improve readability if you do multiple `mutate()` statements to increase clarity for the reader. For instance, in the example below an unfamiliar reader of your code and process would have to check the values for `Sepal.Area` to see if they were based on the original or adjusted `Sepal.Width`. Especially with work that does not

---

[2]This is very similar to what we covered in working with R where you can do `iris$Sepal.Width<-NULL` to remove a column.

need to be highly efficient, it is almost always better to trade
off succinctness/elegance for readability/clarity.

```
iris %>%
  mutate(Sepal.Area = Sepal.Width * Sepal.Length,
    Avg.Sepal.Area = mean(Sepal.Area),
    Sepal.Width=Sepal.Width*.9,
    Sepal.Length=NULL)
```

Sepal.Width	Species	Sepal.Area	Avg.Sepal.Area
3.15	setosa	17.85	17.82287
2.70	setosa	14.70	17.82287
2.88	setosa	15.04	17.82287
2.79	setosa	14.26	17.82287
3.24	setosa	18.00	17.82287
3.51	setosa	21.06	17.82287

7.1 Useful functions

R has lots of functions that you can make use of but I wanted to
call out some specific functions provided by the **tidyverse** that
can come in handy when creating new columns.

We can use **row_number()** to add an ID column to our data.

```
iris %>%
  mutate(id=row_number())
```

Sepal.Length	Sepal.Width	Petal.Length	Petal.Width	Species	id
5.1	3.5	1.4	0.2	setosa	1
4.9	3.0	1.4	0.2	setosa	2
4.7	3.2	1.3	0.2	setosa	3
4.6	3.1	1.5	0.2	setosa	4
5.0	3.6	1.4	0.2	setosa	5
5.4	3.9	1.7	0.4	setosa	6

We can get values from earlier or later rows with **lag()** and **lead()**.
This is particularly useful for comparing values over time.

```
iris %>%
  mutate(prev = lag(Sepal.Length),
         future = lead(Sepal.Length))
```

Sepal.Length	Petal.Width	Species	prev	future
5.1	0.2	setosa	NA	4.9
4.9	0.2	setosa	5.1	4.7
4.7	0.2	setosa	4.9	4.6
4.6	0.2	setosa	4.7	5.0
5.0	0.2	setosa	4.6	5.4
5.4	0.4	setosa	5.0	4.6

The `case_when()` allows us to write a multi-condition statement without nesting lots of `ifelse()` statements. To write a `case_when()` we provide a series of expressions that result in a boolean response and then put the desired label after a tilde (~). The label for the first expression that returns a TRUE gets returned for each row in our dataset. To provide a value that should be returned if no prior condition returns a TRUE, put `TRUE ~ "default label"` as the final condition.

```
iris %>%
  mutate(size = case_when(
    Sepal.Length < mean(Sepal.Length)  ~ "s",
    Sepal.Length > mean(Sepal.Length)  ~ "l",
    TRUE ~ "m"
  ))
```

Sepal.Length	Petal.Width	Species	size
5.1	0.2	setosa	s
4.9	0.2	setosa	s
4.7	0.2	setosa	s
4.6	0.2	setosa	s
5.0	0.2	setosa	s
5.4	0.4	setosa	s

The RHS of the tilde doesn't have to be a fixed value, you can put expressions on the RHS too so long as everything ends up the same datatype.

```
iris %>%
  mutate(Species = case_when(
    Species == "setosa"  ~ toupper(Species),
    TRUE ~ as.character(Species)
  ))
```

Sepal.Length	Petal.Width	Species
5.1	0.2	SETOSA
4.9	0.2	SETOSA
4.7	0.2	SETOSA
4.6	0.2	SETOSA
5.0	0.2	SETOSA
5.4	0.4	SETOSA

There are extra cumulative functions that consider all the rows before the present one. We already have `cumsum()`, `cummin()`, `cummax()` and a few others from base R. `tidyverse` gives us:

- `cumall()` for checking a condition has been TRUE in every prior row
- `cumany()` for checking a condition has been TRUE in any prior row
- `cummean()` for getting the mean of all prior values

The `cumall()` and `cumany()` are especially useful for saying whether things happened in the past, along with `lag()`, as you often want to be able to create such measures as candidate columns when building predictive models.

```
iris %>%
  mutate(runagg=cumall(Sepal.Length<mean(Sepal.Length)))
```

Sepal.Length	Petal.Width	Species	runagg
5.1	0.2	setosa	FALSE
4.9	0.2	setosa	FALSE
4.7	0.2	setosa	FALSE
4.6	0.2	setosa	FALSE
5.0	0.2	setosa	FALSE
5.4	0.4	setosa	FALSE

`mutate()` takes your data, applies the changes, and returns the updated dataset in its entirety. Occasionally, you might want to return only the columns you want to change. In such a situation, swap the word `mutate` for `transmute`.

```
iris %>%
  transmute(Sepal.Width=floor(Sepal.Width),
            Species = case_when(
    Species == "setosa"  ~ toupper(Species),
    TRUE ~ as.character(Species)
  ))
```

Sepal.Width
3
3
3
3
3
3

7.2 Advanced data changes

Like the data manipulation aspects we've already covered, `mutate()` has variants[3] that allow us to perform more programmatic changes to our data.

Using `mutate_all()` you can apply a function to every column.

```
iris %>%
  mutate_all(as.character)
```

Sepal.Length	Sepal.Width	Petal.Length	Petal.Width	Species
5.1	3.5	1.4	0.2	setosa
4.9	3	1.4	0.2	setosa
4.7	3.2	1.3	0.2	setosa
4.6	3.1	1.5	0.2	setosa
5	3.6	1.4	0.2	setosa
5.4	3.9	1.7	0.4	setosa

---

[3]`transmute()` also has these variants.

If you want to change columns where they meet some sort of criteria within the data, you can provide a criteria to `mutate_if()`.

```
iris %>%
    mutate_if(is.numeric, ~ . + rnorm(.))
```

Sepal.Length	Sepal.Width	Petal.Length	Petal.Width	Species
5.801233	4.267989	1.7230783	0.0620613	setosa
4.715885	3.533855	1.7327162	-0.2847584	setosa
4.923484	2.255166	-1.3109879	0.6901706	setosa
5.201911	3.212612	0.3351221	1.7036441	setosa
5.006396	3.135057	1.8885374	0.2789089	setosa
6.924766	3.720268	1.2938308	0.2780320	setosa

To change columns with certain name conditions use the `mutate_at()` variant.

```
iris %>%
    mutate_at(vars(Sepal.Width:Petal.Width), ~ . + rnorm(.))
```

Sepal.Length	Sepal.Width	Petal.Length	Petal.Width	Species
5.1	1.632160	1.5693524	0.1393836	setosa
4.9	2.146251	2.2281803	0.0000095	setosa
4.7	4.762896	-0.6887572	0.3965169	setosa
4.6	3.644356	2.4499652	0.7040535	setosa
5.0	5.181996	1.8891292	-1.3999117	setosa
5.4	1.532164	1.4173460	1.3201975	setosa

7.3 Summary

Use `mutate()` to create, update, or even delete columns from a dataset. Inside a `mutate()` you can perform a mix of all three actions. You can reference columns you're making or updating and R will evaluate those first. You can use `mutate_all()` to apply an update to every column, `mutate_at()` to change columns where the names meet some criteria, and `mutate_if()` to apply an update to only columns that meet some specific criteria based on the data.

7.4 Exercises

1. Create an `irisImperial` dataset with the numeric measurements converted to inches (divide by 2.5), and the Species upper-cased.
2. Add a column to `movies` that says how much the length differs from the median.
3. [ADVANCED] Redo your `irisImperial` code using the `mutate_if()` function to make the conversion more succinct.

Chapter 8

Working with dates and times

This chapter will take you through some of the core functionality you can use so that we can work with datetime columns inside our tables later. The package `lubridate` contains functionality for making dates easy to work with in R.

 Time is one of the quirkiest things you'll ever work with. This covers some fundamentals but there's a huge amount of depth and nuance that could be taken into account. Please give me some feedback[1] if there's something basic that you feel should be included here.

```
library(lubridate)
```

8.1 Date conversions

The first thing that `lubridate` makes it easy to do is to take some strings holding dates and convert these into dates.

`lubridate` gives us conversion functions named after how you expect the order of date and time components to be expressed in the

71

data. If you have a date that has year then month then day you
can use ymd() to convert it. If it then had hours, minutes and
second, the function you need would be ymd_hms().

```
# Not all of these conform to year month day structure
ymd_hms(c("20110604110101","2011-06-04 11:01:01",
          "2011/06/04/11/01/01","2011 june 4th, 11:01:01",
          "2011%06%04%11%01%01","04/06/2011 11:01:01",
          "2011-06-04 11:01:01 PDT",
          "2011-06-04 11:01:00+1400"))
```

```
## [1] "2011-06-04 11:01:01 UTC" "2011-06-04 11:01:01 UTC"
## [3] "2011-06-04 11:01:01 UTC" "2011-06-04 11:01:01 UTC"
## [5] NA                        NA
## [7] "2011-06-04 11:01:01 UTC" "2011-06-03 21:01:00 UTC"
```

lubridate date conversions do have some limitations unfortunately.

- If there are particularly unusual separators then you'll get
  parse problems so you may need to scrub these types of characters first, using some of the string activities in the previous
  chapter.
- This works when everything is in the same order component-
  wise. You can do multiple conversions and use the
  coalesce() function from dplyr to return the first success-
  fully parsed value.
- Time zones must be denoted by using the offset values, not by
  referencing time zone acronyms i.e. in the format [+/-]HHMM
  as opposed to a three letter reference like GMT.

8.2 Date components

R's built-in extractor functions for date components are a little
bit limited. lubridate provides us with many more. Each one
can also be used to set a value if you put it on the LHS of an
assignment.

```
myDate <- ymd_hms("20110604110101")
```

You can extract or set the date component using `date()` function.

```
date(myDate)
date(myDate) <- "2012-05-01"
myDate
```

```
## [1] "2011-06-04"
## [1] "2012-05-01 11:01:01 UTC"
```

Use the `year()` function for extracting or setting the calendar year.

```
year(myDate)
year(myDate) <- year(Sys.Date())
myDate
```

```
## [1] 2012
## [1] "2017-05-01 11:01:01 UTC"
```

Use the `month()` function for extracting or setting the calendar month.

```
month(myDate)
month(myDate) <- month(Sys.Date())
myDate
```

```
## [1] 5
## [1] "2017-12-01 11:01:01 UTC"
```

`lubridate` gives us a number of day functions:

- `yday()` for the number of days into the year
- `mday()` for the number of days into the month
- `wday()` for the number of days into the week
- You can additionally use the arguments `label` and `abbr` to get text labels for the days of the week

```
yday(myDate)
mday(myDate)
wday(myDate)
wday(myDate, label = TRUE, abbr=TRUE)
```

```
## [1] 335
## [1] 1
## [1] 6
## [1] Fri
## Levels: Sun < Mon < Tue < Wed < Thu < Fri < Sat
```

These can also be used to override values. When we override with a value that couldn't exist **lubridate** will roll the date forward by however many days your number exceeds the end of the month by.

```
sept <- ymd("20170903")
mday(sept) <- 31
sept

feb <- ymd("20160204")
mday(feb) <- 31
feb
```

```
## [1] "2017-10-01"
## [1] "2016-03-02"
```

There are also functions for getting and setting time components too.

```
hour(myDate)
minute(myDate)
second(myDate)
```

```
## [1] 11
## [1] 1
## [1] 1
```

8.3   Date arithmetic

You don't usually want to just get and set date attributes, you often want to be able to do date arithmetic where you add some unit of time and get a back a date and/or time that correctly took into account your units given the many, many quirks of our calendar systems.

To do arithmetic with `lubridate` the easiest way to start is with plural versions of the components functions. Functions like `days()` allow to provide the number of days, seconds, or whatever you want to use with your date objects. Once you have some unit described with a plural function, you can then add or subtract it easily.

`myDate`

[1] "2017-12-01 11:01:01 UTC"

`myDate + years(1)`

[1] "2018-12-01 11:01:01 UTC"

`myDate - months(1)`

[1] "2017-11-01 11:01:01 UTC"

`myDate + days(1)`

[1] "2017-12-02 11:01:01 UTC"

`myDate - hours(1)`

[1] "2017-12-01 10:01:01 UTC"

`myDate + minutes(1)`

[1] "2017-12-01 11:02:01 UTC"

`myDate - seconds(1)`

[1] "2017-12-01 11:01:00 UTC"

These work by changing periods and changing values based on the period type and number of periods.

```
feb <- ymd("20160228")
feb + years(1)
```

```
## [1] "2017-02-28"
```

It will not however allow you to create improbable dates e.g. 29th February 2017.

```
feb <- ymd("20160229")
feb + years(1)
```

```
## [1] NA
```

Here is the relevant segment from the `lubridate` documentation, readable via running the command `help("Period-class")`:

> lubridate enforces the reversible property of arithmetic (e.g. a date + period - period = date) by returning an NA if you create an implausible date by adding periods with months or years units to a date. For example, adding one month to January 31st, 2013 results in February 31st, 2013, which is not a real date. lubridate users have argued in the past that February 31st, 2013 should be rolled over to March 3rd, 2013 or rolled back to February 28, 2013. However, each of these corrections would destroy the reversibility of addition (Mar 3 - one month == Feb 3 != Jan 31, Feb 28 - one month == Jan 28 != Jan 31) taking into account many of the rules we expect date arithmetic to adhere to like accounting for leap years.

Sometimes you'll want to use definitions of units of time that aren't based on the calendar year. If you want to use exact duration values e.g. a year being 365 days, as opposed to incrementing the year value, there are functions for this sort of calculation, prefixed with d to denote that you're adding values equivalent to the duration denoted as opposed to incrementing the conceptual value.

```
feb <- ymd("20160228")
feb + years(1)
feb + dyears(1)
```

```
## [1] "2017-02-28"
## [1] "2017-02-27"
```

8.4 Date formatting

Formatting dates for output needs the `format()` function.[2]

```
a_date <- ymd_hms("20160228161101")
format(a_date)
```

```
## [1] "2016-02-28 16:11:01"
```

The `format()` function will output using the format but we can also provide alternative formats. Using alternative formatting involves using components that start with a percentage sign. We can include any other characters we want as delimiters.

```
format(a_date, "%Y yo %m yo %d")
```

```
## [1] "2016 yo 02 yo 28"
```

R gives us a lot of options (read `?strptime` for all of them) but some of the most common formatting strings you're likely to want are:

- `%Y-%m-%d %H:%M:%S` is the default and yields the four digit year, the month with a leading 0, the day with a leading 0, the hour in the 24 hour format, the minute with a leading 0, and the number of seconds with a leading 0.

```
format(a_date, "%Y-%m-%d %H:%M:%S")
```

```
## [1] "2016-02-28 16:11:01"
```

- `%c` will output in your current locale's default

```
format(a_date, "%c")
```

---

[2]Specifically, it requires the `format.date()` or `format.POSIX*()` functions but R will automatically choose these variants when encountering a data type.

```
## [1] "Sun Feb 28 16:11:01 2016"
```

- %D will yield an American style short date format

```
format(a_date, "%D")
```

```
## [1] "02/28/16"
```

- %F will yield the ISO standard date format

```
format(a_date, "%F")
```

```
## [1] "2016-02-28"
```

- %z and %Z allow you to output time zones as either numeric adjustments or time zone abbreviations.

```
format(a_date, "%z")
format(a_date, "%Z")
```

```
## [1] "+0000"
## [1] "UTC"
```

8.5 Common tasks

Outlined here are some **lubridate** based solutions to common date challenges:

- Get the first day of the month for each date.

```
floor_date(ymd("20171009"), "month")
```

```
## [1] "2017-10-01"
```

- Get the last day of the month for each date.

```
ceiling_date(ymd("20171009"), "month") - days(1)
```

```
## [1] "2017-10-31"
```

- Add x months and return the end of the month if month would change due to variable end dates.

```
ymd(c("20171031","20170130")) %m+% months(1)
```

```
## [1] "2017-11-30" "2017-02-28"
```

- Generate a sequence of months. Use the + operator if the value is not going to be a month-end value, otherwise use our operator %m+% to enforce end of month behaviours.

```
ymd("20171011") + months(1:4)
```

```
## [1] "2017-11-11" "2017-12-11" "2018-01-11" "2018-02-11"
```

```
ymd("20171031") %m+% months(1:4)
```

```
## [1] "2017-11-30" "2017-12-31" "2018-01-31" "2018-02-28"
```

- Check if dates are between two other dates

```
ymd(c("20171028","20171031")) %within%
   interval(ymd("20171030"),
            ymd("20171130"))
```

```
## [1] FALSE   TRUE
```

- Check if two date ranges overlap

```
int_overlaps(interval(ymd("20171028"), ymd("20171031")),
             interval(ymd("20171030"), ymd("20171130")))
```

```
## [1] TRUE
```

- Get x weekday of the month.[3]

```
# weekdays run from 1 (Sunday) to 7 (Saturday)
getXthWeekday <- function(ymddatestring, weekday, xth){
  monthStart <- floor_date(ymd(ymddatestring), "month")
```

---

[3]Some alternative solutions are also present in a StackOverflow question[4].

```
  startDay <-  wday(monthStart)
  monthStart+
    days(ifelse(startDay<=weekday,
        weekday-startDay,
        7-(startDay-weekday)
        )) +
    weeks(xth-1)
}

getXthWeekday("20171101", 3, 1)
getXthWeekday("20171101", 3, 2)
getXthWeekday("20171101", 3, 3)
```

```
## [1] "2017-11-07"
## [1] "2017-11-14"
## [1] "2017-11-21"
```

8.6 Summary

Whilst working with dates is pretty hard conceptually, **lubridate** makes it easy to get a lot of the practical work sorted.

Use functions for parsing strings to datetime objects based on the typical structure of the strings. For parsing to date use a combination of y,m, and d e.g. dmy(). If you need to add time to these too then you can add a combination of h,m, and s using an underscore e.g. ymd_hms().

You can get and set components of dates using functions named after the singular for the component you're trying to extract e.g. month().

Perform date arithmetic using functions named after the plural of the component you're trying to add/subtract e.g. months(). These adhere to common expectations but sometimes you need to refer to a component's strict definition e.g. an hour being exactly 60 minutes and ignore the handling of things like daylight's saving time. To use the exact duration functions prefix the plural of the component's name with a d e.g. ddays()

Output dates to conform to expectations in downstream systems or for inclusion in reports using the `format()` function.

8.7 Exercises

1. Get the last day of the previous month for these dates:
   `c("2015, April 29th","2017/01/07","17/08/12")`
2. Dates are hard. Try to get a year and a day from the 29th
   February 2016 using `lubridate` – what do you think the right
   answer should be 1st March 2017 or 2nd March 2017?
3. Generate a sequence of the first day of the month for the next
   36 months.

Chapter 9

Working with text

This chapter will take you through some of the core functionality you can use so that we can work with text inside our tables later.

9.1 Strings

stringr gives us a lot of great functions for working with text data and is geared towards the way we want to work. Functions all start with str_* and all take our strings as the first inputs, making piping a breeze.

```
library(stringr)
```

```
simple <- "This IS HOrribly typed! "
numbers <- c("02","11","10","1")
```

9.1.1 Hunting for values

A core type of task we need to do with strings is finding out whether something we're interested in is present in a string and usually doing something with it if we find it, like replacing it with a new string.

We can use `str_detect()` to get a boolean as to whether a string contains a value.

```
str_detect(simple,"typed")
```

```
## [1] TRUE
```

If we wanted to find and extract some text that matched a pattern, we can use `str_extract()`. In the next example I use `.*` to match any number of characters, as a result the function will return typed and everything in the string after it.

```
str_extract(simple,"typed.*")
```

```
## [1] "typed! "
```

To replace a string we've found, we can use `str_replace*` functions to remove the first instance or all instances of something we're looking for.

```
str_replace(simple, "typed", "written")
str_replace_all(simple, "r", "b")
```

```
## [1] "This IS HOrribly written! "
## [1] "This IS HObbibly typed! "
```

We can also count the number of times a value (or regex pattern) occurs inside strings, using `str_count()`. The next example counts the presence of upper-case and lower-case "i".

```
str_count(simple, "[iI]")
```

```
## [1] 3
```

9.1.2   Regular expressions

In the previous section, I include examples that make use of patterns to hunt down values. This is really powerful because it means I don't have to know all combinations of values upfront – I just have to know what the format is. Patterns and logical conditions that operate over text are **regular expressions** or **regex** for short.

The common things we need to know when we're deciding what we're looking for are:

- whether we expect something to be at the beginning of the string – begin your pattern with ^
- whether we expect something to be at the end of the string – end your pattern with $
- what thing we're looking for
  - anything – put .
  - a known string – use the string but put a \ before any special characters like $ if you want to look for a $
  - one or more of known characters – put the options inside []
  - an alphabetical or numerical range of characters – put inside [] and use a - between the start and end of the range
  - a character of a given type – put type inside [:type:] and type must match a constrained list of options
- how many times we expect it to appear consecutively
  - any number of times – put * after it
  - at least once – put + after it
  - an exact amount – put {n} after it

```
# Extract the first vowel that appears
str_extract(simple, "[aeiou]")
# Extract the first vowel and everything after it
str_extract(simple, "[aeiou].*$")
# Extract all lowercase letters
str_extract_all(simple, "[a-z]")
# Check if string starts with a capital letter
str_detect(simple,"^[A-Z]")
# Check if string ends in punctuation
str_detect(simple,"[:punct:]$")
# Check if `r` appears twice in a row
str_detect(simple, "r{2}")
# Extract where a vowel is followed by a `b`
str_extract(simple,"[aeiou]b")
```

```
## [1] "i"
```

```
## [1] "is IS HOrribly typed! "
## [[1]]
##  [1] "h" "i" "s" "r" "r" "i" "b" "y" "t" "y" "p" "e" "d"
##
## [1] TRUE
## [1] FALSE
## [1] TRUE
## [1] "ib"
```

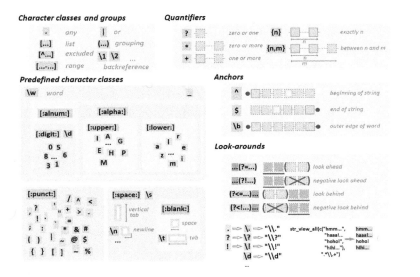

Regular expressions can be incredibly powerful and there are way more options than I've outlined here for constructing patterns. Read ?regex for looking at RegEx supported by R. A neat place to test and learn about regular expressions is regexr.com[1]. The RStudio cheat sheet for working with **stringr** also includes a page of RegEx.

9.1.3 String splitting

We can use **stringr** to break up a string into component strings based on a number of known types of split, or by providing our own custom split points or **delimiters**.

---

[1]https://regexr.com/

String splitting can also be called tokenisation and will be part of a natural language processing book at a later date. That book will also make use of the package `tidytext` for string splitting.

For known types of boundaries like splitting per word or sentence we can use the **boundary()** function to get the criteria needed to split a string that way.

```
str_split(simple, boundary("word"))
str_split(simple, boundary("sentence"))
```

```
## [[1]]
## [1] "This"     "IS"          "HOrribly" "typed"
##
## [[1]]
## [1] "This IS HOrribly typed! "
```

Alternatively, we can provide delimiters ourselves.

```
str_split(simple, "i")
str_split(simple, "[iI]")
```

```
## [[1]]
## [1] "Th"           "s IS HOrr"    "bly typed! "
##
## [[1]]
## [1] "Th"           "s "          "S HOrr"       "bly typed! "
```

9.1.4 Other tasks

Here are a few other tasks you might need to do.

You can change the case of strings using **str_to_*** functions.

```
str_to_lower(simple)
str_to_title(simple)
str_to_upper(simple)
```

```
## [1] "this is horribly typed! "
## [1] "This Is Horribly Typed! "
## [1] "THIS IS HORRIBLY TYPED! "
```

> If you need other ways of manipulating the case of sentences,
> check out the package **lettercase**.

You can remove excess white space characters from the beginning
and end of strings using **str_trim()**.

```
str_trim(simple)
```

```
## [1] "This IS HOrribly typed!"
```

A common difficulty people come across is when numbers have been
stored as text and the values need to be sorted correctly. **stringr**
gives us string specific order and sort functions that we can tell to
process numbers correctly. Use the **order** function when you want
to do things like sort a data.frame the column belongs to, and the
sort function for when you just want some sorted values returned.

```
str_order(numbers, numeric=TRUE)
str_sort(numbers, numeric=TRUE)
```

```
## [1] 4 1 3 2
## [1] "1"  "02" "10" "11"
```

Another common task is finding out how long each string in a
vector is. The function **str_length()** will return a vector holding
the length of each element in a character vector.

```
str_length(numbers)
```

```
## [1] 2 2 2 1
```

9.1.5 Advanced string operations

stringr and some of its operations can make things a little complicated even for experienced R users. For example, if we had a
number of sentences that we split by word we end up with a list

with each element corresponding to the position of the original element in the vector. Each list element contains the results we'd have gotten if we just performed the string function on a sentence by itself.

```
strings <- c("A word","Two words","Not three words")

strings %>%
  str_split(boundary("word"))
```

```
## [[1]]
## [1] "A"     "word"
##
## [[2]]
## [1] "Two"   "words"
##
## [[3]]
## [1] "Not"   "three" "words"
```

If we then wanted to do something that acted on each of the split up words this might not always give us the results we expect.

```
strings %>%
  str_split(boundary("word")) %>%
  str_detect("w")
```

```
## [1] TRUE TRUE TRUE
```

The **stringr** functions are operating on the list and not operating on the bits inside it which is of no use to us. When we want a **stringr** function to be applied to the contents of the list, we can use the **map()** function from **purrr** to make this happen. The **map()** function takes the name of a function we want to apply and any additional arguments we need to pass on.

```
library(purrr)
strings %>%
  str_split(boundary("word")) %>%
  map(str_detect,"w")
```

```
## [[1]]
```

```
## [1] FALSE  TRUE
##
## [[2]]
## [1] TRUE TRUE
##
## [[3]]
## [1] FALSE FALSE  TRUE
```

 Working with lists like this will be covered more extensively in a later book.

9.2 Factors

Factors are a type of text where the number of unique values is fairly low. Common types of factors are state names, countries, survey labels like Agree, medical diagnoses codes, and month names. In such circumstances instead of just recording the text, we can record a number that corresponds to the text. This is more space efficient as numbers take up less memory than text. By using numbers to represent different values, it also gives us a mechanism for providing custom orders to values.

When we make a string, we can just use our `c()` function.

```
myString <- c("red","blue","yellow",NA,"red")
myString
```

```
## [1] "red"    "blue"    "yellow" NA        "red"
```

If we want to make it into a factor, we can use the `factor()` function to convert it.

```
myFactor <- factor(myString)
myFactor
```

```
## [1] red     blue    yellow <NA>    red
## Levels: blue red yellow
```

By default this will extract the unique values, put them in alphabetical order, and then give each one a number. Converting our string puts blue first as a level.

```
levels(myFactor)
```

```
## [1] "blue"   "red"    "yellow"
```

We can remove the text labels from our factors to get the numeric values.

```
as.numeric(myFactor)
```

```
## [1]  2  1  3 NA  2
```

Factors can be handy but they're pretty annoying at times too. They're an area that frequently gets R users into trouble. Thankfully, the **forcats** package makes working with factors much easier. The functions in **forcats** are prefixed with **fct** so it becomes easy to tell when you're working with strings or factors because of the different prefixes involved.

```
library(forcats)
```

You can build a quick frequency table to look at the distribution of values using **fct_count()**.

```
fct_count(myFactor)
```

```
## # A tibble: 4 x 2
##         f     n
##    <fctr> <int>
## 1    blue     1
## 2     red     2
## 3  yellow     1
## 4    <NA>     1
```

You can recode missing values to be their own level in a factor. This makes processing factors easier down the line.

```
fct_explicit_na(myFactor)
```

```
## [1] red        blue        yellow     (Missing) red
## Levels: blue red yellow (Missing)
```

By default factors get assigned levels alphabetically. You can use
`fct_infreq()` to re-order the levels such that they are in frequency
order i.e. the most common value has the lowest level.

```
fct_infreq(myFactor)
```

```
## [1] red     blue    yellow <NA>    red
## Levels: red blue yellow
```

You can combine little used values by using `fct_lump()` to keep the
most common n values or provide a minimum occurrence rate that
must be met for the level to be maintained. Alternatively, you can
provide negative values to lump together the most common values
instead.

```
fct_lump(myFactor, n = 1)
fct_lump(myFactor, prop=.25, other_level = "OTHER")
fct_lump(myFactor, n=-1, other_level = "other")
```

```
## [1] red    Other Other <NA>  red
## Levels: red Other
## [1] red    OTHER OTHER <NA>  red
## Levels: red OTHER
## [1] other  blue    yellow <NA>    other
## Levels: blue yellow other
```

Particularly useful if you want to depersonalise data but still be
able to derive conclusions based on person, **forcats** provides the
`fct_anon()` function to convert values into randomised numeric ID
values. As the results are random, you should put a `set.seed()`
command before you do the anonymisation in order to get consistent results over multiple executions of your code.

```
set.seed(127)
fct_anon(myFactor)
```

```
## [1] 3    1    2    <NA> 3
## Levels: 1 2 3
```

9.3 Summary

The packages **stringr** and **forcats** make it very easy to deal with text data in R. Both packages are installed as part of the **tidyverse** and depending on which version of the tidyverse you have, **stringr** may already be loaded when you use **library(tidyverse)**. They are designed to work in pipelines and have consistent functions that start with **str** for working with strings and **fct** for working with factors.

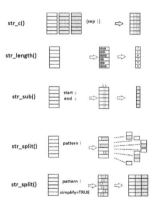

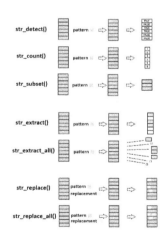

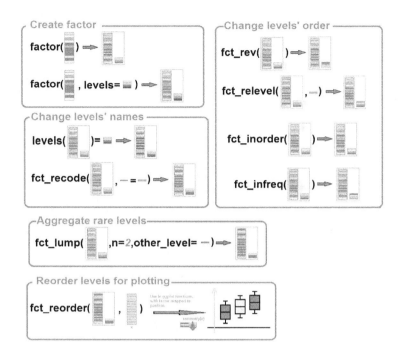

9.4   Exercises

1. Store "the quick brown fox jumps over the lazy dog"
2. Upper case the string
3. [ADVANCED] Split the sentence into words and count the number of letters in each word
4. Count the records in the **gss_cat** dataset by survey year
5. Revise **gss_cat** such that there are only three levels of marital status
6. Race, partyid, religion, and denomination are sensitive values, anonymise them

Chapter 10

Summarising data

10.1 Producing summaries

To aggregate data in our pipelines, we can uses the `summarise()` function. We use this when we want to return a single row with aggregate values, unlike with `mutate()` which will make a new column with the aggregate value repeated in it.

To use `summarise()` provide expressions that result in a single value and provide multiple expressions in a comma separated fashion.

```
iris %>%
  summarise(mean(Sepal.Width), mean(Sepal.Length))
```

mean(Sepal.Width)	mean(Sepal.Length)
3.057333	5.843333

Provide a column title on the LHS of an expression along with an

95

equal sign (=).

```
iris %>%
  summarise(Mean.Sepal.Width=mean(Sepal.Width),
  Mean.Sepal.Length=mean(Sepal.Length))
```

Mean.Sepal.Width	Mean.Sepal.Length
3.057333	5.843333

10.2   Aggregate functions

There are functions like `sum()` and `mean()` that already exist in R but the `tidyverse` gives a number of extra functions that come in handy:

- `n()` to return the number of rows
- `n_distinct()` to return the number of unique values in a column
- `first()`, `last()`, and `nth()` for retrieving values in specific positions in a column

```
iris %>%
  summarise(n = n(), unique= n_distinct(Species),
            first = first(Species), last = last(Species),
            `51st` = nth(Species, 51))
```

n	unique	first	last	51st
150	3	setosa	virginica	versicolor

10.3   Advanced aggregations

You can perform aggregations on all columns using `summarise_all()` and on columns meeting a criteria using `summarise_if()` or `summarise_at()` depending on where the condition you need to check is. These will use the names of the columns being aggregated as the column names for the output.

```
iris %>%
  summarise_all(n_distinct)
```

Sepal.Length	Sepal.Width	Petal.Length	Petal.Width	Species
35	23	43	22	3

```
iris %>%
  summarise_if(is.numeric, mean)
```

Sepal.Length	Sepal.Width	Petal.Length	Petal.Width
5.843333	3.057333	3.758	1.199333

```
iris %>%
  summarise_at(vars(Sepal.Length:Petal.Length), mean)
```

Sepal.Length	Sepal.Width	Petal.Length
5.843333	3.057333	3.758

10.4 Summarising by groups

Most often when performing on analysis we're interested in summary statistics within groups, factors, segments, or cohorts. We can do this using the `group_by()` function. This will provide an instruction to your pipeline that calculations should now be performed within the context of the grouping columns. This means we get summaries per group, do cumulative sums within groups, and more.

We can provide a comma separated list of columns that we want to group by. We can then follow it up with our other functions learnt so far to apply those functions inside each group.

- Produce a summary table

```
iris %>%
  group_by(Species) %>%
  summarise(Avg.Sepal.Length=mean(Sepal.Length))
```

Species	Avg.Sepal.Length
setosa	5.006
versicolor	5.936
virginica	6.588

- Add summary statistics for each group as a column

```
iris %>%
  group_by(Species) %>%
  mutate(Avg.Sepal.Length=mean(Sepal.Length))
```

Sepal.Length	Petal.Width	Species	Avg.Sepal.Length
5.1	0.2	setosa	5.006
7.0	1.4	versicolor	5.936
6.3	2.5	virginica	6.588

- Take records from each group which is useful for getting the first record, especially when used along with sorting

```
iris %>%
  group_by(Species) %>%
  slice(1)
```

Sepal.Length	Sepal.Width	Petal.Length	Petal.Width	Species
5.1	3.5	1.4	0.2	setosa
7.0	3.2	4.7	1.4	versicolor
6.3	3.3	6.0	2.5	virginica

- Perform within group sorting

```
iris %>%
  group_by(Species) %>%
  arrange(desc(Sepal.Length))
```

Sepal.Length	Sepal.Width	Petal.Length	Petal.Width	Species
5.8	4.0	1.2	0.2	setosa
5.7	4.4	1.5	0.4	setosa
7.0	3.2	4.7	1.4	versicolor
6.9	3.1	4.9	1.5	versicolor
7.9	3.8	6.4	2.0	virginica
7.7	3.8	6.7	2.2	virginica

When we perform a `group_by()` the grouping context hangs around. You can replace it with another grouping context to get a different level of aggregation. This is useful if you need to go from a fine grain (lots of rows) aggregation to a low grain (few rows) aggregation or if you need to put various group level metrics against rows.

```
iris %>%
  group_by(Species) %>%
  mutate(SpeciesN=n()) %>%
  group_by(Sepal.Length) %>%
  mutate(Sepal.LengthN=n())
```

Sepal.Length	Petal.Width	Species	SpeciesN	Sepal.LengthN
5.1	0.2	setosa	50	9
4.9	0.2	setosa	50	6
4.7	0.2	setosa	50	2
4.6	0.2	setosa	50	4
5.0	0.2	setosa	50	10
5.4	0.4	setosa	50	6

By default, later groupings override existing groupings but you can use the `add` argument to instead add to the existing grouping context.

```
iris %>%
  group_by(Species) %>%
  mutate(SpeciesN=n()) %>%
  group_by(Sepal.Length, add=TRUE) %>%
  mutate(Sepal.LengthN=n())
```

Sepal.Length	Petal.Width	Species	SpeciesN	Sepal.LengthN
5.1	0.2	setosa	50	8
4.9	0.2	setosa	50	4
4.7	0.2	setosa	50	2
4.6	0.2	setosa	50	4
5.0	0.2	setosa	50	8
5.4	0.4	setosa	50	5

If you need to remove a grouping context to be able to work on the table as a whole again, you can use the **ungroup()** function.

```
iris %>%
  group_by(Species) %>%
  mutate(SpeciesN=n()) %>%
  ungroup() %>%
  head()
```

Sepal.Length	Petal.Width	Species	SpeciesN
5.1	0.2	setosa	50
4.9	0.2	setosa	50
4.7	0.2	setosa	50
4.6	0.2	setosa	50
5.0	0.2	setosa	50
5.4	0.4	setosa	50

10.5   Advanced grouping

We can also perform programmatic groupings. **group_by_all()** can be useful for finding out the number of duplicates in a dataset.

```
iris %>%
  group_by_all() %>%
  summarise(nrows=n())
```

Sepal.Length	Sepal.Width	Species	nrows
4.3	3.0	setosa	1
4.4	2.9	setosa	1
4.4	3.0	setosa	1
4.4	3.2	setosa	1
4.5	2.3	setosa	1
4.6	3.1	setosa	1

group_by_if() allows you to use some criteria for grouping. Useful for if you want to group by text columns, or columns with low uniqueness.

```
iris %>%
  group_by_if(~n_distinct(.)<30) %>%
  summarise(n())
```

Sepal.Width	Petal.Width	Species	n
2.0	1.0	versicolor	1
2.2	1.0	versicolor	1
2.2	1.5	versicolor	1
2.2	1.5	virginica	1
2.3	0.3	setosa	1
2.3	1.0	versicolor	1

group_by_at() allows you to use some criteria for grouping based on names. Useful for if you want to group by columns that have IDs in them for instance.

```
iris %>%
  group_by_at(vars(starts_with("Sp"))) %>%
  summarise(n())
```

Species	n
setosa	50
versicolor	50
virginica	50

10.6 Summary

Produce aggregate rows using the **summarise()** function, or add aggregates to rows using **mutate()**. Use **group_by()** to produce aggregates or perform actions within groups. **group_by()** can be used repeatedly to change the grouping context of activities, and **ungroup()** can remove grouping contexts if required. Programmatic grouping contexts can be generated using **group_by_all()**, **group_by_at()**, and **group_by_if()**.

Hadley Wickham and the other folks who write the code that powers the **tidyverse** are from different places around the world, including places that use British English not American English. As such they very nicely provide British and American variants of function or argument names so you can use what you feel most comfortable with. I'm British so you don't see **summarize()** being used but it is valid. Use whatever you feel comfortable with.

10.7 Exercises

1. Find the min and max values for **length** in **movies**
2. In a pipeline, find out what proportion of films are Action movies, Action Comedies, Comedies, and neither Action or Comedy
3. [ADVANCED] Get the range for each numeric variable in **movies**. Hint: Range outputs two values so you need to make a custom function that will concatenate the outputs of range

Chapter 11

Combining datasets

11.1 Joining two tables to make a wider table

A lot of the time, if we get two datasets we want to combine them based on some criteria to do with columns. For instance, let's say we wanted to analyse sales by customer attributes and we had sales and customer datasets. We would want to match the customer data to the sales data based on the customer identifier so that we could get one dataset where each sales record had customer information as extra columns of data that we could then use to analyse our sales by.

There are different types of joins that we can use. We typically think of our first dataset as our data on the left and the data we are trying to add on as extra columns as being on the right. The different types of joins are:

- **inner join** for getting only rows matched on both sides;

inner join

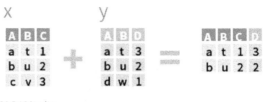

- **left join** for getting all the rows on the left hand side with any matching data from the right;

left join

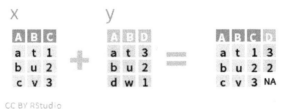

- **full join** for getting all the rows on the left and the right with rows matched where possible;

full join

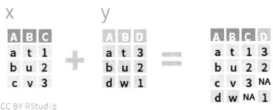

- **anti join** for getting everything on the left where there's no match on the right;
- **cross join** for getting every row on the left joined against every row on the right.

These join types each have an R function, which is the join type with an underscore instead of a space. So **anti join** becomes `anti_join()` and **left join** becomes `left_join()`. At present there is no specific function for performing a `cross_join()` so there is a section in this chapter covering how to do cross joins.

11.1.1 Applying joins to scenarios

Let's explore some scenarios in order to identify the type of join we might use in each case.

- We need to get the sales from registered customers. Here we have sales that may or may not have a customer ID and we want to join our customer data so that it filters out any row which doesn't have a matching customer ID. This would be an *inner join* where we only get rows with matches.
- We need to get the sales with the retail customer or commercial customer details where applicable. In this case, we need to actually get retail data and company data added to our sales data. As we want cases where one or the other are a match, we can't use inner joins as this would filter out non-matches on the first dataset we try so we wouldn't necessarily get any data when we join the second on and we'd lose a lot of sales. Instead, we need to use *left joins* so that we get sales data with customer data where there's a match, and then do the same to get the company data joined onto the sales and customer data where there's a match.
- We need to know how many sales each customer has made, how many customers have not made a sale, and how many sales don't have an associated customer. For this we need to know where customer rows match sales data, where they don't have any corresponding rows in sales, and where there are sales with no match in the customer data. We use a *full join* to get all three types of match i.e. no match on the right, a match on the right, no match on the left.
- We need to provide aggregations about what happened in different categories and times without missing categories or times that had no sales. We can use *cross join* to get every combination of category and time, then *left join* our sales data to this new dataset to ensure we don't miss any categories or times when we do our aggregations.

- We have some text data from customer calls and we want to do some sentiment analysis. We discovered the nifty `tidytext` package and started working through some of the tutorials. One of the `tidytext` functions helped us turn our transcripts into a dataset with each word on its own line. To avoid keeping pointless words around, we then get shown how to do an *anti-join* to remove all the pointless words by comparing our data to the table of stop words. Now we have data fit for sentiment analysis.

11.1.2   Building joins

We need some information for joining data:

- what will be the table that gets joined on to
- what table will be joining onto our first table
- what columns will we use as our match criteria

Our starter table will be mentioned in our main pipeline and then we'll use our table that's joining on to it inside a `*_join()` function. Inside our join, we may also need to provide join criteria if we don't want it to perform matches based on (case-sensitive) name matches.

Let's set up an example. Here I have a table with some colours I want to associate with some species in our `iris` data. Unfortunately, the person who made the table wasn't aware that R is case-sensitive!

```
irisLk <- data_frame(
  species=c("setosa","virginica","VERSICOLOR"),
  colour=c("Red","Blue","Green"))
```

If we want to add the lookup data to our `iris` dataset and we use `left_join()` we'll get an error. This is because the lookup table's species column starts with a lower-case "s".

```
iris %>%
  left_join(irisLk)
```

> Error: `by` required, because the data sources have no common

To specify the join criteria we can pass a vector to the by argument. The vector of our criteria leverages the fact that values in vectors can have names like c("colA"="cola","colB"="colb"). The value on the LHS is the column name from our first table, and the value on the RHS is the column name from the table we're joining to our first table.

```
iris %>%
  left_join(irisLk, c("Species"="species") )
```

Sepal.Length	Petal.Width	Species	colour
5.1	0.2	setosa	Red
4.9	0.2	setosa	Red
7.0	1.4	versicolor	NA
6.4	1.5	versicolor	NA
6.3	2.5	virginica	Blue
5.8	1.9	virginica	Blue

11.1.3 Cross joins

At the time of writing there is no cross_join() function in dplyr which is the primary data manipulation package within the tidyverse.

To perform a cross join we can add a dummy column that will cause a join of every row on the LHS table to every row of the RHS table. We can use some new pipeline syntax which allows us to nest pipelines within each other – using curly braces allows us to provide a multi-line expression as the input to a function argument. Consequently, we're able to provide a version of the irisLk that temporarily has the dummy column at the same time as we're generating the dummy column on our iris table. Once joined, we remove the dummy column using select() as it's no longer required.

```
iris %>%
  mutate(dummycol=1) %>%
  full_join({
    irisLk %>%
      mutate(dummycol=1)
```

```
}, by="dummycol") %>%
select(-dummycol)
```

Sepal.Length	Petal.Width	Species	species	colour
5.1	0.2	setosa	setosa	Red
5.1	0.2	setosa	virginica	Blue
5.1	0.2	setosa	VERSICOLOR	Green
4.9	0.2	setosa	setosa	Red
4.9	0.2	setosa	virginica	Blue
4.9	0.2	setosa	VERSICOLOR	Green

If you find yourself using cross join a lot, you could make a function that makes this process generic.

```
cross_join<-function(x, y){
  x %>%
    mutate(dummycol=1) %>%
    full_join({
      y %>%
        mutate(dummycol=1)
      }, by="dummycol") %>%
    select(-dummycol)
}
```

11.1.4 Join examples

To help get a handle on the different types of joins and the shape of the data they return, let's run through combining **iris** data and the **irisLK** data with our different join types.

If we do a left join, the dimensions of the resulting table are 6 columns which are our original columns plus the extra value column from **irisLk**. Species doesn't need to be replicated multiple times so we don't end up with 7 columns. The row count is 150 as it returns everything from our **iris** table and information from **irisLk** where available.

```
iris %>%
  left_join(irisLk, c("Species"="species"))
```

Sepal.Length	Petal.Width	Species	colour
5.1	0.2	setosa	Red
4.9	0.2	setosa	Red
4.7	0.2	setosa	Red
4.6	0.2	setosa	Red
5.0	0.2	setosa	Red
5.4	0.4	setosa	Red

If we do an inner join, the dimensions of the resulting table are 6 columns like with the left join but now the row count is 100 as it filters out the 50 "versicolor" rows from iris as there's no corresponding row in irisLk.

```
iris %>%
    inner_join(irisLk, c("Species"="species"))
```

Sepal.Length	Petal.Width	Species	colour
5.1	0.2	setosa	Red
4.9	0.2	setosa	Red
4.7	0.2	setosa	Red
4.6	0.2	setosa	Red
5.0	0.2	setosa	Red
5.4	0.4	setosa	Red

Performing a full join gives the amount of columns (6) but returns rows with matches and without from both sides of the join so we end up with 151 rows.

```
iris %>%
    full_join(irisLk, c("Species"="species"))
```

Sepal.Length	Petal.Width	Species	colour
5.1	0.2	setosa	Red
4.9	0.2	setosa	Red
4.7	0.2	setosa	Red
4.6	0.2	setosa	Red
5.0	0.2	setosa	Red
5.4	0.4	setosa	Red

An anti-join filters out cases where there's a match in our join criteria. This doesn't add extra columns so we only have 5 columns, and it filters out the "setosa" and "virginica" rows leaving us with 50 rows.

```
iris %>%
  anti_join(irisLk, c("Species"="species"))
```

Sepal.Length	Sepal.Width	Petal.Length	Petal.Width	Species
7.0	3.2	4.7	1.4	versicolor
6.4	3.2	4.5	1.5	versicolor
6.9	3.1	4.9	1.5	versicolor
5.5	2.3	4.0	1.3	versicolor
6.5	2.8	4.6	1.5	versicolor
5.7	2.8	4.5	1.3	versicolor

A cross join has no concept of a key so it does not de-duplicate columns contained in the join criteria, resulting in 7 columns. It then returns 150 rows from `iris` combined with the 3 rows from `irisLk` such that we end up with 450 rows in total.

```
iris %>%
  cross_join(irisLk)
```

Sepal.Length	Petal.Width	Species	species	colour
5.1	0.2	setosa	setosa	Red
5.1	0.2	setosa	virginica	Blue
5.1	0.2	setosa	VERSICOLOR	Green
4.9	0.2	setosa	setosa	Red
4.9	0.2	setosa	virginica	Blue
4.9	0.2	setosa	VERSICOLOR	Green

11.1.5   Join by position

This isn't something I would generally recommend as data can change order during reruns of queries to databases or users inserting rows in spreadsheets, but you can join data based on position. If you have two data sets of the same number of rows you can use `bind_cols()` to simply combine the two sets of data.

```
iris[,1:3] %>%
  bind_cols(iris[,4:5])
```

Sepal.Length	Sepal.Width	Petal.Length	Petal.Width	Species
5.1	3.5	1.4	0.2	setosa
4.9	3.0	1.4	0.2	setosa
4.7	3.2	1.3	0.2	setosa
4.6	3.1	1.5	0.2	setosa
5.0	3.6	1.4	0.2	setosa
5.4	3.9	1.7	0.4	setosa

11.1.6 Join based on other criteria

You don't always want to join on exact matches of columns. Sometimes you might want to join rows that are earlier than a given date per customer, where values overlap, or where ranges are specified. At the time of writing, this isn't very well supported in the `tidyverse`.

My recommendation right now is to perform a cross join and then use `filter()` to apply your join criteria.

For instance, let's say I want to get get every flower from `iris` and the information about flowers from the same species that are larger than it. I can cross join to get all combinations, then use a filter to ensure they're the same species and add other conditions that enforce the size constraints.

```
iris %>%
  cross_join(iris) %>%
  filter(Species.x == Species.y,
         Sepal.Length.x < Sepal.Length.y,
         Sepal.Width.x  < Sepal.Width.y,
         Petal.Length.x < Petal.Length.y,
         Petal.Width.x  < Petal.Width.y)
```

Sepal.Length.x	Species.x	Sepal.Length.y	Species.y
5.1	setosa	5.4	setosa
5.1	setosa	5.7	setosa
5.1	setosa	5.7	setosa
4.9	setosa	5.4	setosa
4.9	setosa	5.7	setosa
4.9	setosa	5.7	setosa

 These types of joins are much more supported in another data manipulation package called `data.table`. `data.table` will be the subject of a later book. If you find yourself needing higher performance data manipulation or things like complicated joins frequently, I would recommend taking a look at `data.table`.

11.2 Joining two tables to make a longer table

Sometimes we have multiple tables that represent different slices of data. We could have loaded up some different spreadsheet tabs that contain customers from different sources and we need one big customer list, for instance.

11.2.1 Same structure data

The operations that we use if both tables have the same structure are ones that union i.e.. combine two datasets. The `union()` function will de-duplicate results and `union_all()` will return the full set of rows. this means a `union()` result can have fewer rows than the number of rows of the two tables added together, whereas `union_all()` will have exactly the number of rows as the two tables added together.

union

```
iris %>%
  sample_n(50) %>%
  union(sample_n(iris, 75))
```

Sepal.Length	Sepal.Width	Petal.Length	Petal.Width	Species
6.9	3.2	5.7	2.3	virginica
5.1	3.8	1.9	0.4	setosa
5.5	2.3	4.0	1.3	versicolor
6.9	3.1	4.9	1.5	versicolor
7.2	3.6	6.1	2.5	virginica
6.4	3.1	5.5	1.8	virginica

11.2.2 Differing structures

Your data doesn't always have the same structure though – the columns could be jumbled or differ between the data.frames. In such cases, we can use `bind_rows()`. `bind_rows()` matches on column names and will add columns if they weren't present in the first dataset.

bind rows

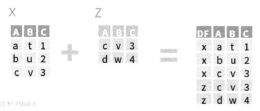

In this example, I take a random sample of 50 records and remove

the Species column. I then use `bind_rows()` to add another 50
rows on to that data only the dataset has all the columns. As a
result, the Species column gets filled with NAs for our first records.

```
iris %>%
  sample_n(50) %>%
  select(-Species) %>%
  bind_rows(sample(iris, 50))
```

Sepal.Length	Sepal.Width	Petal.Length	Petal.Width	Species
6.6	3.0	4.4	1.4	NA
7.2	3.2	6.0	1.8	NA
6.4	2.8	5.6	2.1	NA
4.5	2.3	1.3	0.3	NA
6.4	2.8	5.6	2.2	NA
6.3	2.7	4.9	1.8	NA

If the data is already in R in various objects in memory, you can
add them all to a list and use the `bind_rows()` function to combine
them all in one step.

```
iris1 <- iris[1:50,1:4]
iris2 <- iris[51:100,2:5]
iris3 <- iris[101:150,2:3]

to_merge <- list(iris1, iris2, iris3)

to_merge %>%
  bind_rows() %>%
  nrow()
```

```
## [1] 150
```

11.3 Summary

There's robust techniques for combining multiple datasets into a
single dataset in the `tidyverse` suite of R packages.

- Join two sets of data based on one or more columns such that
  you get all the data from the LHS with matched data from

the RHS using `left_join()`
- Join two sets of data based on one or more columns such that you get only the data from the LHS with matched data from the RHS using `inner_join()`
- Join two sets of data based on one or more columns such that you get all the data from the LHS with matched data from the RHS and rows where there was no match on either side using `full_join()`
- Join two sets of data such that every row from the LHS is matched to every row on the right by creating dummy columns and then performing a different type of join
- Get a dataset with rows removed where there are matches based on one or more columns compared against another dataset using `anti_join()`
- Join two sets of data based on row position using `bind_cols()`
- Combine two datasets of the same structure and remove duplicates using `union()`
- Combine two datasets of the same structure and keep all records using using `union_all()`
- Combine two datasets with varying structures and keep all records using `bind_rows()`
- Combine multiple datasets by adding them to a list and using `bind_rows()`

11.4 Exercises

1. Create a summary of the `movies` data by year that says how many movies were released each year and the average duration
2. Add this summary data to the `movies` table
3. Create a subset of the movies table that has any film over 300 minutes long, use a join to get everything but those records
4. If you didn't do this in an earlier chapter, use `sample_n()` to take a thousand records from `movies`, write the data to CSV with a file name that contains the current time. Rerun the code multiple times to generate some CSVs. Read any CSVs into a combined dataset called `moviessample`

Chapter 12

Reshaping data

Often we get data that has been laid out in ways that make it difficult do analysis. We'll often receive data that has been put into a summary table format and we need to get it into a format so we can do analysis or make charts easily.

Country	2016	2017
UK	5	6
USA	10	8

I would refer to this data as pivoted – there was some data that had row(s) containing a country, a year, and a measure that was pivoted to produce a summary by country and year.

Unpivoting this data involves bringing it back to the country and year level.

Country	Year	Measure
UK	2016	5
UK	2017	6
USA	2016	10
USA	2017	8

Once data is unpivoted, we can do a lot more calculations without having to do anything complex. This is great when we're working with our data. Once we've produced some summaries, we'll then need to pivot the data again for presentation purposes.

12.1   Unpivoting data

To go from pivoted data, we can use the **gather()** function as in "you gather up all the data". When we **gather()** the data, we need to provide the destination with column names for the old column names and the cell contents. Optionally, we can provide specifications as to which columns we want included or excluded from the action – we usually want to avoid unpivoting the ID columns for instance.

Let's use our **mtcars** data with the row names converted to a column.

```
mtcars %>%
  rownames_to_column("car")  ->
  mtcars2
```

car	mpg	cyl	disp	hp	drat	wt	qsec
Mazda RX4	21.0	6	160	110	3.90	2.620	16.46
Mazda RX4 Wag	21.0	6	160	110	3.90	2.875	17.02
Datsun 710	22.8	4	108	93	3.85	2.320	18.61
Hornet 4 Drive	21.4	6	258	110	3.08	3.215	19.44
Hornet Sportabout	18.7	8	360	175	3.15	3.440	17.02
Valiant	18.1	6	225	105	2.76	3.460	20.22

To unpivot this data, we say what our destination column should be for our old column headers, the column name for our pivoted values, and we can also provide inclusions or exclusions for stuff we don't want to be unpivoted. In the case of **mtcars2**, I want to retain the car against every measure.

```
mtcars2 %>%
  gather(measure, value, -car)
```

car	measure	value
Mazda RX4	mpg	21.0
Mazda RX4 Wag	mpg	21.0
Datsun 710	mpg	22.8
Hornet 4 Drive	mpg	21.4
Hornet Sportabout	mpg	18.7
Valiant	mpg	18.1

The data in this layout is great for analysing. For instance, if I need to know the difference from mean for each car and measure combo, I can now use groupby() and mutate() to achieve this.

```
mtcars2 %>%
  gather(measure, value, -car) %>%
  group_by(measure) %>%
  mutate(diff= value-mean(value))
```

car	measure	value	diff
Mazda RX4	mpg	21.0	0.909375
Mazda RX4 Wag	mpg	21.0	0.909375
Datsun 710	mpg	22.8	2.709375
Hornet 4 Drive	mpg	21.4	1.309375
Hornet Sportabout	mpg	18.7	-1.390625
Valiant	mpg	18.1	-1.990625

As well the optional inclusion and exclusion of columns, you can also specify how to handle missings (na.rm), whether to change datatype from character (convert) if you have numeric column names for instance, and if you want the column names to end up stored as a factor (factor_key).

```
mtcars2 %>%
  gather(measure, value, -car, factor_key=TRUE)
```

car	measure	value
Mazda RX4	mpg	21.0
Mazda RX4 Wag	mpg	21.0
Datsun 710	mpg	22.8
Hornet 4 Drive	mpg	21.4
Hornet Sportabout	mpg	18.7
Valiant	mpg	18.1

12.2   Pivoting data

Going from a long view of our data to a wider one involves using the spread() function, which spreads our data out over multiple columns. To spread() data we need to say which column will become our column names and which values will go into our cells. Ideally, you should not have duplicate combinations of values which will stay on the rows and those that will become column names. In such cases it's often best to perform an aggregation step first.

For instance, let's get a table that shows the average miles per gallon (mpg) split out by whether cars are automatic (am) and the number of cylinders (cyl).

```
mtcars2 %>%
  group_by(cyl, am) %>%
  summarise(avg=mean(mpg)) %>%
  spread(am, avg)
```

cyl	0	1
4	22.900	28.07500
6	19.125	20.56667
8	15.050	15.40000

There aren't formatting options that you can apply when pivoting data so you need to format data whilst it's in a long form. Common formatting you may want to apply include:

- scales::percent()[1] function from the package scales al-

---

[1] The percent() function is from the scales package. Here I use the package::function() notation to use a function from a package without running library().

lows nice percent based formatting
- `round()` allows you do typical rounding activities
- `format()` allows you to format value, for instance; including thousand delimiters
- `paste`, `paste0`, and `str_c()` from `stringr` allow you to combine values

```
mtcars2 %>%
  group_by(cyl, am) %>%
  summarise(avg=round(mean(mpg),1)) %>%
  spread(am, avg)
```

cyl	0	1
4	22.9	28.1
6	19.1	20.6
8	15.1	15.4

Other options include what do when data is missing for a given combination of row and column (`fill`), allow the changing of datatypes (`convert`), reduce factors (`drop`), or include the column name as a prefix to the new columns (`sep`).

```
mtcars2 %>%
  group_by(cyl, am) %>%
  summarise(avg=round(mean(mpg),1)) %>%
  spread(am, avg, sep=":")
```

cyl	am:0	am:1
4	22.9	28.1
6	19.1	20.6
8	15.1	15.4

12.3 String splitting revisited

In an earlier chapter we covered various way of splitting strings. They're not necessarily optimised for working in data.frames though. Inside the package `tidyr` is another string splitting function called `seperate()` that we can use instead. This is very handy when you want to convert a column in a dataset into multiple columns.

To use **seperate()** you provide the column you'd like to split and the new column names desired in a vector. This means you should have an expectation about how the columns will end up – other string splitting methods might be more appropriate when you don't know in advance.

```
data_frame(measure=c("net 2017","gross 2017")) %>%
    separate(measure,c("type","year"))
```

type	year
net	2017
gross	2017

Optional arguments you can use include what to separate on (**sep**), clean up (**remove**), how to handle data types (**convert**), and what behaviour should occur when you were wrong about the splits (**extra**).

```
data_frame(measure=c("net 2017","gross 2017")) %>%
    separate(measure,c("type","year"),
             convert=TRUE, remove=FALSE)
```

measure	type	year
net 2017	net	2017
gross 2017	gross	2017

12.4   Summary

Unpivot a dataset using the **gather()** function. Provide it with the destination column names for the repeated measures and the values. Add in references columns you want to include or exclude from the transformation.

Pivot a dataset using the **spread()** function. Provide it with the repeated value column to be used as destination column names and the column that will populate the table cells. Prior to using `spread()` remove extraneous columns that can screw up your transformation. Pre-format the values that will go into the cells.

Transform a column to multiple column when data is consolidated using the `seperate()` function. Provide it with the column to be split, a vector of new column names, and optionally what separator to use.

12.5 Exercise

1. Unpivot the `who` dataset, keeping everything from country to year on each row
    - Use string manipulation to change `newrel` to `new_rel` in what used to be column names
    - Use `seperate()` to split out the measure components as much as possible
2. Make a table showing country population as a percentage of global population by year using the `population` dataset
    - Calculate the percentage of the worlds population by year for each country
    - Format the percentage
    - Excluding columns as required, pivot the data

Chapter 13

Getting data out of R

Like the chapter on getting data, this chapter does not exhaustively cover working with different data stores. The focus in this chapter is writing data to CSVs, spreadsheets, and databases.

13.1 CSVs

You can write a dataset to CSV using the `write_csv()` function in `readr`. Generally, packages that do write activities in the `tidyverse` will follow this convention of `write_filetype()` which will make it easier for you to pick up further capabilities when working with files.

By default, `write_csv()` only needs two arguments:

- a dataset
- a destination file name

```
write_csv(iris, "iris.csv")
```

The destination file name can also include information about where the file should be stored.

- If you just put `"filename.csv"` then the file will be stored wherever R is currently working.

- Look at the location mentioned next to the Console header for insight into where its currently working. This is hopefully inside a project directory.
- Alternatively, you can run `getwd()` to get the information.

- If you put `"./filename.csv"` the file will be written in the current directory as the . denotes the current directory.
- If you put `"../filename.csv"` the file will be written to the directory above the one R is currently working in.
- If you put `"~/filename.csv"` the file will be stored in your home directory. The tilde (~) represents your user home directory.
- In Windows, your home directory is usually "My documents".
- In Linux and Mac, your home directory is your user account's root directory.
- RStudio will do code completion for file structures which can make it easy to specify where to save things.

You can also provide much more detail if you have requirements that are not met by the defaults.

- Specify how missing values should be encoded in the file with the `na` argument
- Add date to an existing file instead of overwriting it if it exists by using the `append` argument
- Specify whether to add column names with the `col_names` argument

If you need a different delimiter to a comma, `write_delim()` will allow you to provide a delimiter.

13.2   Spreadsheets

The simplest way to start writing data to a spreadsheet is with the package `writexl`. This gives us a very simple write experience and resulting output. It's cross-platform and has no external dependencies.

```
library(writexl)
write_xlsx(iris, "iris.xlsx")
```

The only optional argument for `write_xlsx()` is column names. This package is intentionally simple and light.

If you need a more configurable write to Excel, you can use `openxlsx`. It's cross-platform with no external dependencies either but is substantially slower than writexl[1].

```
library(openxlsx)
write.xlsx(iris, "iris.xlsx")
```

The tweaking of parameters allows you to a fairly wide variety of work, including setting the sheet name, setting the output up as an Excel table, and specifying it's location on the sheet.

```
write.xlsx(iris, "iris.xlsx",
           sheetName="iris",
           asTable=TRUE,
           startCol=2, startRow=2)
```

If you need even more complicated writes then you'll need one of the packages like **writeXL** that depend on Java.[2]

13.3 Databases

Using our database connection we can write data new or existing tables in the database.

```
dbConn<-dbConnect(odbc(),
           driver="ODBC Driver 13 for SQL Server",
           server="mhknbn2kdz.database.windows.net",
           database="AdventureWorks2012",
           uid="sqlfamily",
           pwd="sqlf@m1ly")
```

The function for writing data to the database is `dbWriteTable()`. This takes a database connection, a table name, and the data you want written to the database. Optional arguments include:

---

[1]Benchmark provided by Jeroen Ooms in *The writexl package: zero dependency xlsx writer for R* snip.ly/benchmark

[2]I would recommend pushing back on such requirements as much as possible!

- **overwrite** to drop existing data and insert new data
- **append** to insert data into an existing table
- **field.types** to provide specific data types instead of relying on auto-detection

```
dbWriteTable(dbConn,
             "iris",
             iris,
             overwrite=TRUE)
```

13.4 Summary

This chapter covered how to write data to CSV, Excel, and to a database. The packages I recommend you get started with are **readr**, **readxl**, and **writexl**. These all follow the convention of **action_file()** which makes it easy to remember what you need to do.

13.5 Exercises

2. Write the dataset **movies** to CSV
3. Write the dataset **movies** to a spreadsheet
4. Use **sample_n()** to take a thousand records from **movies**, write the data to CSV with a file name that contains the current time.

Chapter 14

Putting it all together

If you're not experienced at manipulating data, the stuff we've covered so far can feel disconnected. Each section shows building block that you can use to make really powerful data pipelines but it can be difficult to see how you can piece them all together. This section provides a rough workflow for you to go through when performing some data manipulation and works through some examples. It then has exercises that you can tackle to help you put things into practice like you would in the wild.

The flowchart here is not exhaustive of all cases but is a great framework to help you get started in building data pipelines.

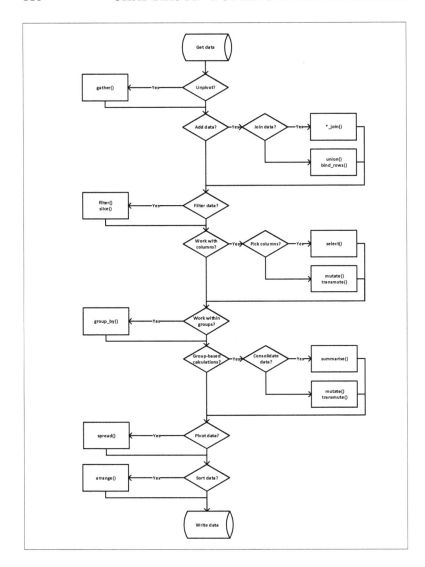

14.1   Working with the `flights` data

We'll start by solving the sorts of questions or requests you might answer using the `flights` data from `nycflights13`

```
library(nycflights13)
```

14.1.1 How many flights arrived late each month?

Before we even begin answering this, the first thing we need to know is what does the person mean by late?[1] Asking the person who made the request we find out a plane arrives late if it arrives more than 5 minutes after its scheduled arrival time.

Thinking about this in the context of the flowchart:

- our data is `flights`

```
flights
```

- we don't need to unpivot our data
- we don't need to add data
- we were not given any specific time ranges so no filtering required
- we already have month in our data so we don't need to do any work with columns
- we need to work within a group of **month**

```
flights %>%
  group_by(month)
```

- we need a group-based calculation that consolidates data by sums the instances where flights are late
    - after investigating the data we see NAs in the arr_delay column we need to remove

```
flights %>%
  group_by(month) %>%
  summarise(lateflights=sum(arr_delay>5, na.rm=TRUE))
```

---

[1]You might also want to ask what they mean by month but we'll leave it as calendar month for simplicity here.

month	lateflights
1	8988
2	8119
3	9033
4	10544
5	8490

- we don't need to pivot the data as we're only analysing by a single dimension

14.1.2 What percentage of traffic did each carrier represent, by month?

- our data is `flights`

`flights`

- we don't need to unpivot our data
- we don't need to add data
- we were not given any specific time ranges so no filtering required
- we already have month and carrier in our data so we don't need to do any work with columns
- we need to work within a group of `month` and `carrier` to be able to get the lowest level of information we need

```
flights %>%
  group_by(month, carrier)
```

- we need a group-based calculation that counts the number of rows per group

```
flights %>%
  group_by(month, carrier) %>%
  summarise(n=n())
```

month	carrier	n
1	9E	1573
1	AA	2794

- we need to work within a group of `month` to compare `carrier` flight counts to the total for each month

```
flights %>%
  group_by(month, carrier) %>%
  summarise(n=n()) %>%
  group_by(month)
```

- we need a within group calculation that compares each carrier's monthly volume to the total monthly volume

```
flights %>%
  group_by(month, carrier) %>%
  summarise(n=n()) %>%
  group_by(month) %>%
  mutate(prop=n/sum(n))
```

month	carrier	n	prop
1	9E	1573	0.0582506
1	AA	2794	0.1034662

- we need to pivot the data as we're analysing by two dimensions
- our proportion needs to be formatted first with `scales::percent()`
- we won't need our `n` field so we should remove that in our `mutate()`

```
flights %>%
  group_by(month, carrier) %>%
  summarise(n=n()) %>%
  group_by(month) %>%
  mutate(prop=scales::percent(n/sum(n)),
         n=NULL) %>%
  spread(month, prop)
```

carrier	1	2	3	4
9E	5.8%	5.8%	5.6%	5.3%
AA	10.3%	10.1%	9.7%	9.6%
AS	0.2%	0.2%	0.2%	0.2%
B6	16.4%	16.4%	16.5%	15.9%
DL	13.7%	13.8%	14.5%	14.4%

14.1.3   What was the latest flight to depart each month?

- our data is `flights`

`flights`

- we don't need to unpivot our data
- we don't need to add data
- we were not given any specific time ranges so no filtering required
- we already have month and departure delay in our data so we don't need to do any work with columns
- we need to work within a group of `month` to be able to get find the flight with the longest delay in each month

```
flights %>%
  group_by(month)
```

- we need to identify which flight had the largest delay, we can do this by sorting

```
flights %>%
  group_by(month) %>%
  arrange(desc(dep_delay))
```

year	month	day	dep_time	sched_dep_time	dep_delay
2013	1	9	641	900	1301
2013	6	15	1432	1935	1137

- we can now use `slice()` to get the first row for each group which gives us the record with the greatest departure delay by month

```
flights %>%
  group_by(month) %>%
  arrange(desc(dep_delay)) %>%
  slice(1)
```

year	month	day	dep_time	sched_dep_time	dep_delay
2013	1	9	641	900	1301
2013	2	10	2243	830	853

14.2 Working with the gapminder data

This section looks at answering some questions about population based on the **gapminder** dataset

```
library(gapminder)
```

14.2.1 What data was excluded to make the gapminder dataset?

The person who made the datasets didn't document the difference between `gapminder` and `gapminder_unfiltered`.[2] Before we can draw conclusions from the data we need to know what is removed so we can understand if we want to rely on the data.

We should run some sort of summary on our datasets first.

- our first dataset is **gapminder** and our bigger dataset is `gapminder_unfiltered`

```
gapminder
gapminder_unfiltered
```

---

[2] Jenny Bryan is awesome so of course she did but if it were some data produced in your organisation you might not know the rules that made it if documentation is missing or hard to find so we're playing make believe here.

- we don't need many of the things that we could do – we just
  need to consolidate to a single row with the number of unique
  values for each column (initially)

```
gapminder %>%
  summarise_all(n_distinct)
```

```
gapminder_unfiltered %>%
  summarise_all(n_distinct)
```

country	continent	year	lifeExp	pop	gdpPercap
142	5	12	1626	1704	1704

country	continent	year	lifeExp	pop	gdpPercap
187	6	58	2571	3312	3313

- visually inspecting those, the main difference looks to be the
  number of years in each dataset
- starting with our **gapminder_unfiltered** dataset let's work-
  out which years have data

```
gapminder_unfiltered
```

- we can join our **gapminder** data on with a left join to get
  where there's matches

```
gapminder_unfiltered %>%
  left_join(gapminder)
```

country	continent.x	year	lifeExp.x	pop.x	gdpPercap.x
Afghanistan	Asia	1952	28.801	8425333	779.4453
Afghanistan	Asia	1957	30.332	9240934	820.8530

- we can group our data by **year** to be able to produce summaries

```
gapminder_unfiltered %>%
  left_join(gapminder) %>%
  group_by(year)
```

- we can summarise per year how many records there are in the unfiltered dataset (all rows) and how many there are in the filtered dataset (no NAs in the *.y columns)

```
gapminder_unfiltered %>%
  left_join(gapminder)   %>%
  group_by(year) %>%
  summarise( unfiltered=n(),
             filtered= sum(!is.na(pop.y)))
```

year	unfiltered	filtered
1950	39	0
1951	24	0
1952	144	142
1953	24	0
1954	24	0

It looks like there are a number of years with much smaller amounts of data and have been excluded as a consequence.

14.2.2 Is there data for every key year for all countries?

We noticed there are still some records for key years that didn't make it into the filtered dataset – we should check that at least the data for the countries that did make it is available for every year.

- we get our **gapminder** data
- we group by country and then we can write a summary that says how many records they have and we can also write a check to ensure there are no duplicates

```
gapminder %>%
  group_by(country)   %>%
  summarise(years=n(), years_check= n_distinct(year))
```

country	years	years_check
Afghanistan	12	12
Albania	12	12

- we can now write some checks to verify that every country has the same number of records and that there aren't duplicates

```
gapminder %>%
  group_by(country)  %>%
  summarise(years=n(), years_check= n_distinct(year)) %>%
  filter( years != max(years) | years != years_check) %>%
  nrow()
```

```
## [1] 0
```

14.2.3   Provide an indexed GDP based on the earliest data

Indexing values means expressing it as the proportion of a baseline value. As a result, we need to get the earliest data and use that to divide each record's GDP against that value where the country matches.

- we start with our **gapminder** data
- we need to filter to the earliest year and keep these as our base values

```
gapminder %>%
  filter(year==min(year)) %>%
  select(year, base=gdpPercap) ->
  index_vals
```

year	base
1952	779.4453
1952	1601.0561

- we can now add this base value as a new column by joining the **index_vals** data onto **gapminder**

```
gapminder %>%
  inner_join(index_vals)
```

```
## Joining, by = "year"
```

country	year	lifeExp	pop	gdpPercap	base
Afghanistan	1952	28.801	8425333	779.4453	779.4453
Afghanistan	1952	28.801	8425333	779.4453	1601.0561

- we can now calculate the indexed GDP

```
gapminder %>%
  inner_join(index_vals) %>%
  mutate(indexedgdp=gdpPercap/base)
```

```
## Joining, by = "year"
```

country	year	gdpPercap	base	indexedgdp
Afghanistan	1952	779.4453	779.4453	1.000000
Afghanistan	1952	779.4453	1601.0561	0.486832

14.3 Exercises

It's now your turn to practice going from question to answer! Good luck.

1. Which carrier had the largest percentage of flights that departed late in the `flights` data?
2. Show flights by carrier to different destinations
3. What is the average flight speed (distance travelled divided by time spent in the air) for each carrier?
4. Does the average flight speed vary by distance to the destination?
5. Show the average life expectancy by continent over time based on the `gapminder` data
   - Account for population by country
6. What is the actual change in population for countries over time in the `gapminder` data

Chapter 15

Conclusion

This book covered some of the fundamentals of data manipulation, from importing data, to working with strings and dates, to slicing and dicing tabular data like a pro. These are fundamental skills that you need to nail. There's some other data structures and formats that I haven't covered that are fairly important. Most of these will get dedicated treatment in later books.

15.1   The tidyverse

We used the `tidyverse` extensively in this book. Running `library(tidyverse)` loads packages for importing data, manipulating data, and writing data pipelines. These are core requirements to most analytical projects you will need to do. If you need to load up individual packages, the vital ones are:

- `dplyr` for core data manipulation
- `tidyr` for pivoting and unpivoting data
- `stringr` for text manipulation
- `forcats` for working with factors
- `readr` for reading flat files
- `readxl` for reading Excel data
- `magrittr` gives you the data pipeline operator (`%>%`) although many packages will load this up for you

A lot of these packages have some nifty cheat sheets produced by

RStudio on rstudio.com[1]. These are really handy to keep printed out and to hand.[2]

15.2 Stepping through the workflow

Your typical steps through basic data analysis will involve

- importing data using functions like `read_csv()` and `read_excel()`
  - use the `map_df()` function as a wrapper around these read functions to read and combine data from multiple sources
  - use the `bind_rows()` function to combine data from multiple datasets in memory
- using `spread()` and `gather()` to reshape data as required
- cleaning data using `filter()` and `mutate()` to remove rows and change or create columns
  - use variants ending with `all`, `if`, and `at` to avoid repetitive typing
- combining multiple datasets of related information using the various join functions
- analysing data by group using `group_by()` and add within group aggregates using `mutate()` to the data or condense data by using `summarise()`
  - use variants ending with `all`, `if`, and `at` to avoid repetitive typing

The next steps are building plots (covered in book 3), reports (probably book 4), working with different data stores (probably book 5), and models (later books).

15.3 Thank you

Thank you all for reading the book and I hope it's been useful to you! Please leave a review on Amazon to help others decide if this book is right for them.

---

[1]https://www.rstudio.com/resources/cheatsheets/
[2]As well as this book, obviously!

Chapter 16

Answers

16.1 Piping

- Write a pipeline that samples from the vector **LETTERS** 200 times and stores the result in a vector called **lots_of_LETTERS**

```
LETTERS %>%
  sample(200, replace = TRUE) ->
  lots_of_LETTERS
```

- Write a pipeline that provides upper-cased versions of the column names of the dataset **mtcars**

```
mtcars %>%
  colnames() %>%
  toupper()
```

```
## [1] "MPG"  "CYL"  "DISP" "HP"   "DRAT" "WT"   "QSEC" "VS"
```

16.2   Filtering columns

- Write a `select()` that gets from the `movies` data (from `ggplot2movies`) the columns `title` through to `votes`, and `Action` through to `Short`

```
movies %>%
  select(title:votes, Action:Short)
```

title	year	length	budget	rating
$	1971	121	NA	6.4
$1000 a Touchdown	1939	71	NA	6.0
$21 a Day Once a Month	1941	7	NA	8.2
$40,000	1996	70	NA	8.2
$50,000 Climax Show, The	1975	71	NA	3.4
$pent	2000	91	NA	4.3

- Write a query that brings back the `movies` dataset without any column that begins with `r` or `m`

```
movies %>%
  select(starts_with("r"),starts_with("m"))
```

rating	r1	r2	r3	r4
6.4	4.5	4.5	4.5	4.5
6.0	0.0	14.5	4.5	24.5
8.2	0.0	0.0	0.0	0.0
8.2	14.5	0.0	0.0	0.0
3.4	24.5	4.5	0.0	14.5
4.3	4.5	4.5	4.5	14.5

- [ADVANCED] Write a query that returns columns that have a high degree of missing data (more than 25% of rows are NA) from the `movies` dataset

```
movies %>%
  select_if(~sum(is.na(.))/length(.)>.25)
```

budget
NA
NA
NA
NA
NA
NA

16.3 Filtering rows

- Write a filter that gets all action movies the `movies` dataset from the **ggplot2movies** package

```
movies %>%
  filter(Action==1)
```

title	year	length	budget	rating
$windle	2002	93	NA	5.3
'A' gai waak	1983	106	NA	7.1
'A' gai waak juk jaap	1987	101	NA	7.2
'Crocodile' Dundee II	1988	110	NA	5.0
'Gator Bait	1974	88	NA	3.5
'Sheba, Baby'	1975	90	NA	5.5

- Write a filter that removes films lasting more than 6 hours from the `movies` dataset

```
movies %>%
  filter(length<6*60)
```

title	year	length	budget	rating
$	1971	121	NA	6.4
$1000 a Touchdown	1939	71	NA	6.0
$21 a Day Once a Month	1941	7	NA	8.2
$40,000	1996	70	NA	8.2
$50,000 Climax Show, The	1975	71	NA	3.4
$pent	2000	91	NA	4.3

- [ADVANCED] Write a filter that checks to see if any of the films don't have any genres flagged at all

```
movies %>%
    filter_at(vars(Action:Short), all_vars(.==0))
```

title	year	length	budget	rating
$50,000 Climax Show, The	1975	71	NA	3.4
'49-'17	1917	61	NA	6.0
'94 du bi dao zhi qing	1994	96	NA	5.9
'Gator Bait II: Cajun Justice	1988	95	NA	3.1
'Hukkunud Alpinisti' hotell	1979	80	NA	7.7
'I Do...'	1989	86	NA	6.2

16.4   Working with names

- Output the `movies` dataset with the column `budget` changed to `budget_if_known`

```
movies %>%
    rename(budget_if_known=budget)
```

title	year	length	budget_if_known	rating
$	1971	121	NA	6.4
$1000 a Touchdown	1939	71	NA	6.0
$21 a Day Once a Month	1941	7	NA	8.2
$40,000	1996	70	NA	8.2
$50,000 Climax Show, The	1975	71	NA	3.4
$pent	2000	91	NA	4.3

- [ADVANCED] Write a query that returns from the `movies` dataset columns that have a high degree of missing data (more than 25% of rows are NA) and upper case all the output column names

```
movies %>%
    select_if(~sum(is.na(.))/length(.)>.25, str_to_upper)
```

BUDGET
NA
NA
NA
NA
NA
NA

16.5   Re-arranging your data

- Sort the `movies` data by title in descending order

```
movies %>%
  arrange(desc(title))
```

title	year	length	budget	rating
Zzyzx	2005	90	1e+06	8.0
Zzim	1998	101	NA	4.5
Zzikhimyeon jukneunda	2000	94	NA	4.7
Zywot Mateusza	1967	80	NA	5.4
Zyosyuu syukeininn Maria	1995	75	NA	3.7
Zyklus von Kleinigkeiten	1999	86	NA	6.0

- [ADVANCED] Sort the `movies` data by columns containing only two unique values

```
movies %>%
  arrange_if(~n_distinct(.)==2)
```

title	year	length	budget	rating
$50,000 Climax Show, The	1975	71	NA	3.4
'49-'17	1917	61	NA	6.0
'94 du bi dao zhi qing	1994	96	NA	5.9
'Gator Bait II: Cajun Justice	1988	95	NA	3.1
'Hukkunud Alpinisti' hotell	1979	80	NA	7.7
'I Do...'	1989	86	NA	6.2

16.6   Changing your data

- Create an `irisImperial` dataset with the numeric measurements converted to inches (divide by 2.5), and the Species upper-cased.

```
iris %>%
  mutate(Species=toupper(Species),
         Sepal.Width=Sepal.Width/2.5,
         Sepal.Length=Sepal.Length/2.5,
         Petal.Width=Petal.Width/2.5,
         Petal.Length=Petal.Length/2.5)
```

Sepal.Length	Sepal.Width	Petal.Length	Petal.Width	Species
2.04	1.40	0.56	0.08	SETOSA
1.96	1.20	0.56	0.08	SETOSA
1.88	1.28	0.52	0.08	SETOSA
1.84	1.24	0.60	0.08	SETOSA
2.00	1.44	0.56	0.08	SETOSA
2.16	1.56	0.68	0.16	SETOSA

- Add a column to `movies` that says how much the length differs from the median

```
movies %>%
  mutate(median_diff=length-median(length))
```

title	year	length	budget	median_diff
$	1971	121	NA	31
$1000 a Touchdown	1939	71	NA	-19
$21 a Day Once a Month	1941	7	NA	-83
$40,000	1996	70	NA	-20
$50,000 Climax Show, The	1975	71	NA	-19
$pent	2000	91	NA	1

- [ADVANCED] Redo your `irisImperial` code using the `mutate_if()` function to make the conversion more succinct.

```
iris  %>%
  mutate(Species=toupper(Species))%>%
  mutate_if(is_numeric, ~./2.5)
```

Sepal.Length	Sepal.Width	Petal.Length	Petal.Width	Species
2.04	1.40	0.56	0.08	SETOSA
1.96	1.20	0.56	0.08	SETOSA
1.88	1.28	0.52	0.08	SETOSA
1.84	1.24	0.60	0.08	SETOSA
2.00	1.44	0.56	0.08	SETOSA
2.16	1.56	0.68	0.16	SETOSA

16.7 Working with dates

- Get the last day of the previous month for these dates: c("2015, April 29th","2017/01/07","17/08/12")

```
c("2015, April 29th","2017/01/07","17/08/12") %>%
  ymd() %>%
  floor_date(.,unit = "month") - days(1)
```

```
## [1] "2015-03-31" "2016-12-31" "2017-07-31"
```

- Dates are hard. Try to get a year and a day from the 29th February 2016 using **lubridate** – what do you think the right answer should be 1st March 2017 or 2nd March 2017?

```
dmy("29th February 2016") + dyears(1) + days(1)
```

```
## [1] "2017-03-01"
```

- Generate a sequence of the first day of the month for the next 36 months.

```
ceiling_date(Sys.Date(),unit = "month") + months(0:35)
```

```
## [1] "2018-01-01" "2018-02-01" "2018-03-01" "2018-04-01"
```

16.8   Working with strings

- Store "the quick brown fox jumps over the lazy dog"

```
font_string<-"the quick brown fox jumps over the lazy dog"
```

- Upper case the string

```
font_string %>%
  str_to_upper()
```

```
## [1] "THE QUICK BROWN FOX JUMPS OVER THE LAZY DOG"
```

- Split the sentence into words and count the number of letters in each word

```
font_string %>%
  str_split(boundary("word")) %>%
  map(str_length)
```

```
## [[1]]
## [1] 3 5 5 3 5 4 3 4 3
```

- Count the records in the `gss_cat` dataset by survey year

```
gss_cat$year %>%
  factor() %>%
  fct_count()
```

```
## # A tibble: 8 x 2
##        f      n
##    <fctr> <int>
## ## 1    2000   2817
## ## 2    2002   2765
## ## 3    2004   2812
## ## 4    2006   4510
## ## 5    2008   2023
## ## 6    2010   2044
## ## 7    2012   1974
## ## 8    2014   2538
```

- Revise `gss_cat` such that there are only three levels of marital status

```
gss_cat$marital<-fct_lump(gss_cat$marital,2)
```

- Race, partyid, religion, and denomination are sensitive values, anonymise them

```
gss_cat$race<-fct_anon(gss_cat$race)
gss_cat$relig<-fct_anon(gss_cat$relig)
gss_cat$denom<-fct_anon(gss_cat$denom)
gss_cat$partyid<-fct_anon(gss_cat$partyid)
```

16.9 Summarising data

- Find the min and max values for `length` in `movies`

```
movies %>%
  summarise(min=min(length), max=max(length))
```

min	max
1	5220

- In a pipeline, find out what proportion of films are Action movies, Action Comedies, Comedies, and neither Action or Comedy

```
movies %>%
  group_by(Action, Comedy) %>%
  summarise(n=n()) %>%
  mutate(prop=n/sum(n))
```

Action	Comedy	n	prop
0	0	37605	0.6951017
0	1	16495	0.3048983
1	0	3912	0.8344710
1	1	776	0.1655290

- [ADVANCED] Get the range for each numeric variable in `movies`. Hint: Range outputs two values so you need to make a custom function that will concatenate the outputs of range

```
movies %>%
  summarise_if(is.numeric,
              ~paste(range(., na.rm=TRUE),
                     collapse = "-"))
```

year	length	budget	rating	votes
1893-2005	1-5220	0-200000000	1-10	5-157608

16.10   Combining datasets

- Create a summary of the `movies` data by year that says how many movies were released each year and the average duration

```
movies %>%
  group_by(year) %>%
  summarise(n=n(),avg_length=mean(length)) ->
  movies_sum
```

- Add this summary data to the `movies` table

```
movies %>%
  inner_join(movies_sum)
```

Joining, by = "year"

title	year	length	n	avg_length
$	1971	121	646	92.97214
$1000 a Touchdown	1939	71	484	64.22107
$21 a Day Once a Month	1941	7	521	66.30326
$40,000	1996	70	1390	85.92806
$50,000 Climax Show, The	1975	71	619	93.68174
$pent	2000	91	2048	79.16943

- Create a subset of the movies table that has any film over 300 minutes long, use a join to get everything but those records

```
movies %>%
  filter(length>=300) ->
  long_movies
```

```
movies %>%
  anti_join(long_movies)
```

title	year	length	budget	rating
$	1971	121	NA	6.4
$1000 a Touchdown	1939	71	NA	6.0
$21 a Day Once a Month	1941	7	NA	8.2
$40,000	1996	70	NA	8.2
$50,000 Climax Show, The	1975	71	NA	3.4
$pent	2000	91	NA	4.3

- Use `sample_n()` to take a thousand records from `movies`, write the data to CSV with a file name that contains the current time. Rerun the code multiple times to generate some CSVs. Read any CSVs into a combined dataset called `moviessample`.

```
movies %>%
  sample_n(1000) %>%
  readr::write_csv(.,
                   paste0("movies",
                          format(now(), "%Y%m%d%H%M%S"),
                          ".csv"))

list.files(pattern = "movies") %>%
  map_df(read_csv) ->
  moviessample
```

16.11   Reshaping data

- Unpivot the `who` dataset, keeping everything from country to year on each row
  - Use string manipulation to change `newrel` to `new_rel` in what used to be column names
  - Use `seperate()` to split out the measure components as much as possible

```
who %>%
  gather("key","value",-(country:year)) %>%
  mutate(key=str_replace(key,"newrel","new_rel")) %>%
  separate(key, c("type","measure","genderage")) %>%
  separate(genderage,c("gender","age"),sep=1)
```

country	iso2	iso3	year	type
Afghanistan	AF	AFG	1980	new
Afghanistan	AF	AFG	1981	new
Afghanistan	AF	AFG	1982	new
Afghanistan	AF	AFG	1983	new
Afghanistan	AF	AFG	1984	new
Afghanistan	AF	AFG	1985	new

- Make a table showing country population as a percentage of global population by year using the `population` dataset
  - Calculate the percentage of the worlds population by year for each country
  - Format the percentage
  - Excluding columns as required, pivot the data

```
population %>%
  group_by(year) %>%
  mutate(prop=scales::percent(
    population / sum(as.numeric(population),
                     na.rm=TRUE))) %>%
  select(year, country, prop) %>%
  spread(year, prop)
```

country	1995	1996	1997	1998
Afghanistan	0.3%	0.3%	0.3%	0.3%
Albania	0.1%	0.1%	0.1%	0.1%
Algeria	0.5%	0.5%	0.5%	0.5%
American Samoa	0.0%	0.0%	0.0%	0.0%
Andorra	0.0%	0.0%	0.0%	0.0%
Angola	0.2%	0.2%	0.2%	0.2%

16.12 Getting data out of R

- Install and load the package `ggplot2movies`

```
if(!require("ggplot2movies")) install.packages("ggplot2movies")
library(ggplot2movies)
```

- Write the dataset `movies` to CSV

```
readr::write_csv(movies, "movies.csv")
```

- Write the dataset `movies` to a spreadsheet

```
writexl::write_xlsx(movies, "movies.xlsx")
```

- Read the data from the spreadsheet into an object called `movies2`

```
movies2<-readxl::read_excel("movies.xlsx")
```

- Use `sample_n()` to take a thousand records from `movies`, write the data to CSV with a file name that contains the current time.

```
movies %>%
  sample_n(1000) %>%
  readr::write_csv(., paste0("movies",
                             format(now(), "%Y%m%d%H%M%S"),
                             ".csv"))
```

16.13   Putting it all together

- Which carrier had the largest percentage of flights that departed late in the `flights` data?

```
flights %>%
  group_by(carrier) %>%
  summarise(late_flights = sum(dep_delay>5, na.rm = TRUE),
            flights = n(),
               late_flights_prop= late_flights/flights) %>%
  slice(which.max(late_flights_prop))
```

carrier	late_flights	flights	late_flights_prop
F9	278	685	0.4058394

- Show flights by carrier to different destinations

```
flights %>%
  group_by(carrier, dest) %>%
  summarise(flights = n()) %>%
  spread(carrier, flights, fill = "")
```

dest	9E	AA	AS	B6	DL
ABQ				254	
ACK				265	
ALB					
ANC					
ATL	59				10571
AUS	2	365		747	357

- What is the average flight speed (distance travelled divided by time spent in the air) for each carrier?

```
flights %>%
  group_by(carrier) %>%
  summarise(avg_speed = sum(distance, na.rm = TRUE) /
               sum(air_time, na.rm=TRUE)) %>%
  arrange(desc(avg_speed))
```

carrier	avg_speed
HA	7.997269
VX	7.483497
AS	7.428769
UA	7.330243
AA	7.271611
DL	7.188905

- Does the average flight speed vary by distance to the destination?

```
flights %>%
  group_by(dest) %>%
  summarise(avg_speed=sum(distance, na.rm = TRUE) /
            sum(air_time, na.rm=TRUE)) %>%
  filter(avg_speed!=Inf) %>%
  mutate(mean=mean(avg_speed), diff=avg_speed-mean) %>%
  arrange(desc(avg_speed))
```

dest	avg_speed	mean	diff
JAC	8.444084	6.773326	1.670758
BQN	8.175209	6.773326	1.401883
ANC	8.157337	6.773326	1.384011
PSE	8.152115	6.773326	1.378789
SJU	8.137829	6.773326	1.364503
HNL	8.122526	6.773326	1.349200

- Show the average life expectancy by continent over time based on the gapminder data
    - Account for population by country

```
gapminder %>%
  mutate(sum_lifeExp=lifeExp*pop) %>%
  group_by(continent,year) %>%
  summarise(avg_lifeExp= round(
    sum(as.numeric(sum_lifeExp), na.rm=TRUE)/
    sum(as.numeric(pop), na.rm=TRUE),2)) %>%
  spread(continent, avg_lifeExp)
```

year	Africa	Americas	Asia	Europe
1952	38.80	60.24	42.94	64.91
1957	40.94	62.02	47.29	66.89
1962	43.10	63.44	46.57	68.46
1967	45.18	64.51	53.88	69.55
1972	47.21	65.70	57.52	70.47
1977	49.21	67.61	59.56	71.54

- What is the actual change in population for countries over time in the gapminder data

```
gapminder %>%
  group_by(country) %>%
  arrange(year) %>%
  mutate(diff=pop-lag(pop))
```

country	continent	year	lifeExp	diff
Afghanistan	Asia	1952	28.801	NA
Afghanistan	Asia	1957	30.332	815601
Afghanistan	Asia	1962	31.997	1026149
Afghanistan	Asia	1967	34.020	1270883
Albania	Europe	1952	55.230	NA
Albania	Europe	1957	59.280	193808

www.ingramcontent.com/pod-product-compliance
Lightning Source LLC
LaVergne TN
LVHW022320060326
832902LV00020B/3581